the Rules of Love

STERLING and the distinctive Sterling logo are registered trademarks of Sterling Publishing Co., Inc.

Library of Congress Cataloging-in-Publication Data Available

10 9 8 7 6 5 4 3 2 1

a ravenous book

Produced by Hollan Publishing, Inc.
100 Cummings Center, Suite 125G
Beverly, MA 01915
© 2008 by Hollan Publishing, Inc.

Published by Sterling Publishing Co., Inc.
387 Park Avenue South, New York, NY 10016
Distributed in Canada by Sterling Publishing
c/o Canadian Manda Group, 165 Dufferin Street
Toronto, Ontario, Canada M6K 3H6
Distributed in the United Kingdom by GMC Distribution Services
Castle Place, 166 High Street, Lewes, East Sussex, England BN7 1XU
Distributed in Australia by Capricorn Link (Australia) Pty. Ltd.
P.O. Box 704, Windsor, NSW 2756, Australia

The Producer maintains the records relating to images in this book required by 18 USC 2257 which records are located at
Hollan Publishing, Inc., 100 Cummings Center, Suite 125G, Beverly, MA 01915.

Printed in Thailand

Sterling ISBN-13: 978-1-4027-4932-2
ISBN-10: 1-4027-4932-5

For information about custom editions, special sales, premium and
corporate purchases, please contact Sterling Special Sales
Department at 800-805-5489 or specialsales@sterlingpublishing.com.

Photography by Allan Penn
Cover and interior design by Amy Sly

the *Rules* of *Love*

THE 64 ARTS OF THE
Kama Sutra

SUZIE HEUMANN

STERLING/RAVENOUS
An imprint of Sterling Publishing Co., Inc.

New York / London
www.sterlingpublishing.com

*To erotic explorers
everywhere*

Contents

Introduction

Nowhere, and at no other time in the history of the world, has there been a book quite like the *Kama Sutra*. This book is synonymous with the erotic skills and exotic passion that we crave and imagine for our own lives. Having no equivalent for today's lovers, we turn to this love manual, this ancient book, for our instruction in the "Rules of Love."

This book on *Kama*, or pleasure, crafted so wisely by its original author, was designed as a love, courtship, and sex manual. The *Kama Sutra* is easy to understand although some of the language is a bit archaic. It was written in short phrases, or *sutras*, so it could be interpreted by those assigned to educate the next generation of young lovers. It is a book that over the millennia was distilled from its original, longer verses down to the essence of knowledge that people might need to conduct themselves wisely in matters of love.

In the twenty-first century, new versions of the *Kama Sutra* have been created for our more modern society. Some parts of the *Kama Sutra*, though very detailed and extensive, don't exactly coalesce with today's morals, practices, and culturally accepted relationships. Many of the extensive chapters involve the details of marrying multiple wives; strange, outdated courting customs; undocumented and bizarre aphrodisiac substances; and almost tribal-like "reconfigurations" of genital parts. Whereas this information may be of interest to some people, it is not the substance of what is generally thought of as the *Kama Sutra*, and most of it is inapplicable to Western society.

The sixty-four arts of the *Kama Sutra* will be illuminated for you in these pages. You'll find the original twenty-four *Kama Sutra* positions here in addition to forty more from such famed erotic manuals as the *Ananga Ranga* and the *Perfumed Garden*. Sixty-four detailed positions plus a few extras will whet your erotic appetite for inspired and breathtaking sex. Passages from the original manuscript and details from modern science and body/mind philosophy are combined to present the best of the ancient and the new.

Although the *Kama Sutra* has been quoted and interpreted many times before, you will find an entirely new version in *The Rules of Love*. Through exquisite photography, new commentary, and profound practices, you'll find everything that you need to enhance and inform your love life. As you try the positions and engage in love practices that expand your pleasure, know that you are now traveling a road that will lead to wondrous ecstasy, an erotic dimension that you previously thought existed only in your dreams.

1

The Book of Love

"The followers of the Babhravya school of thought enumerate eight stages during the union: Embracing, Kissing, Marking with nails, Marking with teeth, Uniting in congress, Shrieking and crying, The woman assuming the role of the man, and Oral congress. Each of these is supposed to have eight subdivisions, making a total of sixty-four."

—Part 1, Chapter 2, Verses 5-6, the *Kama Sutra*

HOW THE BOOK OF LOVE CAME TO BE

The erotic ideas and passionate lessons you find in the *Kama Sutra* are thousands of years old. Originally passed down through oral traditions, the *Kama Sutra* we know today has been condensed from a much older Sanskrit manuscript—the *Kama Shastra*—some time between the first and fourth centuries A.D. The original Shastras (sciences) were about one thousand chapters long.

The *Kama Sutra*'s author was a man named Vatsyayana. An ascetic and scholar, Vatsyayana compiled the *Kama Sutra* and included his own opinions and ideas as he wrote. For example, he added a more liberal understanding of human nature: "Even those embraces that are not mentioned in the *Kama Sutra* should be practiced at the time of sexual enjoyment, if they are in any way conducive to the increase of love and passion. Texts on the science of Kama are of help only until passion is excited; but once the wheel of passion begins to roll, there is no sutra and no order." (Part 2, Chapter 2, Verses 31–32 the *Kama Sutra*)

THE SUTRAS TO LIVE LIFE BY

During the time of Vatsyayana's life, a good citizen of India was expected to know many diverse things. The sciences were well advanced and intricately woven together to form a complete picture of universal understandings. Rigorous health practices, a basic knowledge of the laws and books of the times, an understanding of the universe and its workings, a grasp of the physical sciences, and knowledge of the Hindu rituals honoring the gods and goddesses were all expected of well-bred people.

The trilogy of the *Artha Sutra*, *Dharma Sutra*, and *Kama Sutra* comprised the universal ideas and concepts that ruled the lives of the people of ancient India. The *Artha Sutra* is about the acquisition of material goods and the pursuit of economic interests. *Artha* is the first objective of life because one cannot pursue the others, *Dharma* and *Kama*, without wealth, a home, and a business. *Artha* includes acquisition of art, land, gold, cattle, wealth, equipment, and friends. The *Dharma Sutra* is about right action in life, including worship and deity reverence, family honoring, community service, and moral obligations. The *Kama Sutra*, the third part of the trilogy, is about the pursuit of all things pleasurable, which includes sexuality. Sex was very important, but it was not taken out of context from the cultural whole that included the concepts of Artha and Dharma and all the other aspects of pleasure that the *Kama Sutra* covers.

If a good citizen learned and followed these things faithfully, then his life would progress well and the number of lifetimes he was destined to live could be shortened. He would escape the cycle of death and rebirth much sooner if he were virtuous in these prescribed ways. To achieve *Nirvana*, the heavenly realm at the end of the soul's cycle of life, was, and is, the goal of all Hindus.

Sexuality, and the union created by it, was a metaphor for the union between human beings and the whole of the universe. The Hindu pantheon of gods and goddesses enacted the depth of this idea. Shiva, the male principle of the universe, and Shakti, the female principle, came together to form the whole of creation. Shiva is the active principle, the sustaining element that brings consciousness to our existence. Shakti is the female principle and the initiator in sex and life. She holds birth, death, and redemption in her hands. Shiva and Shakti cannot exist without each other. The yin-yang symbol is representative of the union of Shiva and Shakti: the Union of the Cosmos.

A LOOK AT ANCIENT HINDU SOCIETY

India has always been a highly structured society. The caste system has influenced and guided India for hundreds of centuries. High caste people were, and are to this day, well educated and culturally refined. Certain castes have certain privileges, while other castes have different ones. Though the caste system has many destructive aspects, historically it gave members of each of the castes a certain pride in their own rights and privileges.

The *Kama Sutra* provides detailed instructions not only about cultural topics but also about personal activities such as daily cleanliness ("Bathing should be a daily affair; limbs must be massaged on alternate days; every third day soap must be applied to the thighs"), when eating should occur ("Meals should be taken in the forenoon and the afternoon"), when to shave ("Every fourth day the face must be shaved") and cut the hair, what to wear and what not to wear, what one should do in the evening for entertainment, and so forth. Although it was generally thought that parents would naturally teach these things to their children, nothing was left to chance. An orderly existence was one of the ways societal forces kept individuals controlled.

The Art of Love

Kama translates to "pleasure"– pleasure of all kinds, including enjoying the arts and sciences, games, family and friends, nature, and sensual and sexual exploits. *Sutra* means "aphorisms" or "short verses." Its distillation of the teachings of the *Kama Shastras* helped spread and sustain these principles throughout the culture because the short sayings could be easily remembered and interpreted by experts of the day.

Gender differences were very strong in Indian society during this time. Men had many exclusive privileges that would today seem unfair and misogynous. Life for women in the higher castes—the Brahman, king, and warrior castes—was highly structured. Women were sheltered and protected as they cultivated the home arts, raised children, spent time in a small circle of other women and children, cooked, sewed, studied the fine arts, and were generally confined to very close quarters. Men made the decisions, ran the businesses, worshiped outside the home, went to parties and public performances, traveled, and were otherwise very worldly and active. In the *Kama Sutra* there are many references to evening activities when men and courtesans would meet for parties, gaming, conversation, dancing, and more. No women from any households could attend.

RICHARD BURTON, TRANSLATOR

Sir Richard Burton is credited with being the translator and illuminator of the *Kama Sutra* for the Western world. His assistant, fact-finder, and collaborator in the translations was a man named Foster Arbuthnot. While Arbuthnot did the majority of the rough translating, it was Burton who brought the manuscript to light and oversaw its transformation for English society.

Richard Burton is not only famous for the fabulous historical books he discovered but also for his many adventures. He is credited with knowing forty languages and was a scholar and an intrepid traveler, in addition to being an enlisted man in the Bombay Native Infantry in India. Burton is acclaimed as being the first white explorer to travel up the Nile River in Africa to look for the source of the Nile. He refused to go any further after the expedition came to Lake Tanganyika, so his fellow explorer, John Speke, continued on to eventually discover Lake Victoria, the real source of the Nile. So although Burton was not credited with that discovery, he was its inspiration.

Defying religious and moral prescriptions, Burton was known to disguise himself and enter Muslim holy grounds and pilgrimage places where white men were prohibited. He is reported to have learned about the Eastern sexual arts through the women he encountered while in India. He was often described as looking like a vagabond and beggar more than a member of English society. His very Catholic and pious wife, Isabel, whom he left in England, contrasted with his wild and ambitious life in the Orient.

In 1883, Burton formed the Kama Shastra Society in London and published the first version of the *Kama Sutra*. There were only a handful of members and only a thousand copies printed, but word soon spread of its titillating text. The *Kama Sutra* was a shock to the very prudish Victorian society of the time.

Burton went on to translate the *Ananga Ranga* (1885), the *Perfumed Garden* (1886), the *1,001 Arabian Nights* tales, and many other historic volumes from Sanskrit and Arabic into English by the time of his death in 1890. On the evening before his death he completed the last chapter of the *Perfumed Garden*, a chapter that had been left out of the original publication by the Kama Shastra Society. It contained the parts on homosexuality and pederasty. The day he died his very conservative wife burned more than a thousand pages in a fire. She then proceeded to burn all of his unpublished manuscripts. Many are completely lost and have never been translated to this day.

THE OTHER BOOKS OF LOVE

While many books on sexuality and erotica exist in our contemporary society, love explorers of the past had their own versions of erotica. In addition to the *Kama Sutra*, several other books that have been translated from Sanskrit and Arabic contain sensual and sexual content that corroborates, supports, and expands upon the more well-known teachings. China, Japan, and other Eastern cultures had sexual and intimacy instructional manuals such as the *Ishimpo*, *Secrets of the Jade Bed Chamber*, and other "pillow books" to titillate, instruct, and arouse ancient lovers.

THE ANANGA RANGA

The *Ananga Ranga* is also from India and was written sometime during the sixteenth century, much later than the *Kama Sutra*. It is much more rigid than the *Kama Sutra*, though it does address the woman's importance in lovemaking, reflecting trends that had changed things over the centuries. It details the importance of pelvic floor muscle control of the woman so that she can affect and heighten the experience with her lover. Cleanliness, seduction, creating potions and aphrodisiacs, being adept at many positions, rituals, magic spells, morality, and feminine prowess are covered. It is certain that Taoist influences informed the content of the *Ananga Ranga*.

THE PERFUMED GARDEN

The *Perfumed Garden* is another book from the sixteenth century and is Arabian in origin. In addition to sexual position instruction, it extensively covers the ideology and descriptions of thirty-five different penis sizes and thirty-eight different vagina types. How, why, and when these different genital types come together in lovemaking was of great importance in the various erotic manuals of history. Using teaching stories, the *Perfumed Garden* provides instruction to the man to ask his lover how to pleasure her so that she is satisfied.

"We have a little collection of classic lovemaking books that we keep on a shelf by the bed. Sometimes we'll just pick up one of them, when we're looking for something new, and point to a random page. But what really turns me on is when I see my wife in bed, reading one and smiling, I know we're in for a session of hot sex!"

—William, 34

The Art of Love

"Lingam" refers to the phallus, which is worshiped as a symbol of the Hindu god Shiva, and throughout the *Kama Sutra* refers to a man's penis. "Yoni" refers to the vulva, which is worshiped as a symbol of the Hindu goddess Shakti, and throughout the *Kama Sutra* refers to a woman's vagina.

SECRETS OF THE JADE BED CHAMBER

The best-known erotic manual from China is *Secrets of the Jade Bed Chamber*. Influenced by Taoism, it includes potency remedies, positions, thrusting patterns, genital typing, relationship counseling, feminine sexual secrets, and empowerment of the female in lovemaking technique and sentiment. Like many sexual "languages" of ancient Eastern philosophy, symbolism is artfully used in this book. Word plays such as "jade garden" or "jade gate" for the vagina, and "jade stalk" for the penis, are understood throughout Arabic, Sanskrit, Japanese, and Chinese languages.

ISHIMPO

The *Ishimpo*, a Taoist sex manual, is part of the oldest surviving set of medical transcripts from Japan. It was written in the tenth century and is very extensive. The *Ishimpo* is styled in a dialogue-type writing structure that is used in many manuals, erotic and otherwise, from Eastern cultures. The female principle speaks to the male principle in the form of questions, answers, and discourse.

THE YIN-YANG SYMBOL

The yin-yang symbol comes from the Taoism, which influences all Eastern cultures. The male/female nature is symbolic of the reality of all of nature. Thus, sexual union was and is seen as the union of all opposites and the unification of all worldly parts. Sex between men and women was understood to control the very universe—it literally made the world go round.

EASTERN SEX MANUALS

Eastern sex manuals had names such as *Sex Handbook of the Dark Girl*, *Discourse of the Plain Girl*, and *Nine Spirits of Women*. Much power was granted to women in these cultures, as initiator and sexual seducer. These "pillow books" were considered educational. They consisted of erotic paintings, drawings, and text that would excite lovers as they lay in bed and approached lovemaking.

"The *Kama Sutra has so many interesting ideas besides sex positions. My boyfriend was really surprised the first time I scratched his shoulder and now he knows just how to nibble my thighs to drive me wild!"*

–Kris, 29

THE PARTS AND MEANINGS OF THE *KAMA SUTRA*

The *Kama Sutra* is written in seven parts, each according to different aspects of the conduct of love. While Westerners primarily think of the *Kama Sutra* as a manual of exotic sexual positions, it also presents details on many other aspects of the intimate dance that thrives between lovers of all kinds, although some are no longer pertinent in today's world. Nonetheless, it is the world's best-known erotic instruction book.

THE SIXTY-FOUR ARTS OF THE *KAMA SUTRA*

In the *Kama Sutra* there are two loosely structured sets of instructions. There are the sixty-four arts and sciences that citizens are encouraged to learn, of which sexuality is one, and there are the sixty-four sexual arts. Eight times eight is sixty-four—this is a magical formula formed by the sets of eight.

The more a person knew of the first set of sixty-four, the more attractive he or she became and the more desirable for marriage. This set includes things like astrology and astronomy, cooking, food preservation and the making of elixirs, game playing and word play, crafting flower arrangements and the making of garlands for religious icons and rituals, proper deity honoring, sexual skills, business skills, medicine preparation, singing, dancing, instrument playing, and so on. The more skills a person knew, the cleverer he was considered to be and the more admirers he would supposedly have. His company would be sought after in society and good things would come to him.

The second set of sixty-four has to do with sexuality, though not only positions.

There are actually only twenty-four positions described in the Kama Sutra. They are divided into one set of eight for general uniting in sexual congress, another set for the woman assuming the role of the man, and a set for oral sex—the first three of eight sets. Then there are eight types of scratching, eight types of biting, eight types of kissing, eight types of embracing, and eight ways to make noise during sexual play—for a total of sixty-four combinations for the sex act.

PART 1: AN INTRODUCTION FROM THE *KAMA SUTRA*

> *"On the acquisition of obtaining Dharma, Artha, and Kama: Man, the period of whose life is one hundred years, should practice Dharma, Artha, and Kama at different times and in such a manner that they may harmonize together and not clash in any way."*
> —Part 1, Chapter 2, the Kama Sutra

Part one of the *Kama Sutra* covers general remarks on the life and goals of the citizen. It is prescribed that a good citizen be well educated in the rules and morals of behavior of the times and of the Hindu holy rites. These include acquiring knowledge, obtaining wealth (Artha), following the ethics and principles of community and religious life (Dharma), and following the practices that assure a pleasurable life existence (Kama).

The Art of Love

The word *congress* is used to describe intercourse in the *Kama Sutra*. It is a formal term and its greater meaning implies a meeting for a special purpose—much as erotic lovemaking can be.

PART 2: ON SEXUAL UNION

"The kinds of sexual union according to the dimensions, force of desire, or passion and time. Man is divided into three classes; the hare man, the bull man, and the horse man, according to the size of his lingam. Woman also, according to the depth of her yoni, is either a female deer, a mare, or a female elephant."
—Part 2, Chapter 1, the Kama Sutra

Part two of the *Kama Sutra* is called "amorous advances" or "sexual union," depending on the translation. It is for this section that the *Kama Sutra* is most famous, although in fact it is a very small part of the complete book. However, because it is the sexual positions in the *Kama Sutra* that people in the modern world seem most able to relate to, the Rules of Love will focus extensively on these positions. Additional parts in this section include embracing, kissing, biting, caressing, positions, oral sex, scratching, love marks, desire, the behavior of women, and the beginning and ending of a lovemaking session.

PART 3: ABOUT THE ACQUISITION OF A WIFE

"When a girl of the same caste, and a virgin, is married in accordance with the precepts of the Holy Writ, the results of such a union are the acquisition of Dharma and Artha. . . . For this reason a man should fix his affections upon a girl who is of good family."
—Part 3, Chapter 1, the Kama Sutra

Part three is on acquiring a wife. The *Kama Sutra* details the rituals involved in courting and relaxing the girl, the different forms a marriage can take, seduction, convincing a girl to marry you, approaching a man in public, designing time to be in the same space as the one you love, finding a go-between, and all of the other skills required in the fine art of being a successful suitor. It also discusses abduction, forcing sex, love triangles, and clearing one's good name after an adverse event.

PART 4: ABOUT A WIFE

"A virtuous woman, who has affection for her husband, should act in conformity with his wishes as if he were a divine being. . . . She should keep the whole house well cleaned, and arrange flowers of various kinds in different parts of it, and make the floor smooth and polished so as to give the whole a neat and becoming appearance."
—*Part 4, Chapter 1, the* **Kama Sutra**

Part 4 of the *Kama Sutra* details the duties and privileges of a wife and how she should conduct her life. Besides keeping the household, a wife's duties included tending a garden filled with herbs and flowers for ceremonial honoring of the deities. She prepared all of the items required for the morning, afternoon, and evening offerings to the gods and goddesses. The expert handling of these religious duties was said to win the heart of a potential husband beyond all other things.

This part of the *Kama Sutra* also addresses the issues of being the only wife in a household and the situations where she might be the first wife of several, or even a second or third wife. Each position has its place and certain actions and privileges. Commentary is included on suggestions for a peaceful and harmonious harem life and how each wife should conduct herself.

> *"My husband is a rather large man (in all places!), and I'm kind of small, which means we can't do everything in the Kama Sutra—but some of the more unusual positions we've learned allow us to go on and on and on for long nights of erotic passion."*
> *–Lynn, 37*

PART 5: ABOUT THE WIVES OF OTHER PEOPLE

"The wives of other people may be resorted to on the occasions . . . but the possibility of their acquisition, their fitness for cohabitation, the danger to oneself in uniting with them, and the future effect of these unions, should first of all be examined."
—*Part 5, Chapter 1, the* **Kama Sutra**

Having an affair with another man's wife has a prescribed conduct, though counsel is against men doing this. How to conduct oneself, how to set up an encounter, how to use an intermediary, when it is advised not to engage in extramarital affairs, and what sort of women are more inclined to it are all covered. In some parts of India, at the time of the *Kama Sutra*'s writing, kings had the right and privilege to deflower young brides—anyone's bride, for that matter—so this subject is also covered.

PART 6: ABOUT COURTESANS

"By having intercourse with men, courtesans obtain sexual pleasure, as well as their own maintenance. Now when a courtesan takes up with a man for love, the action is natural; but when she resorts to him for the purpose of getting money, her action is artificial or forced."
—*Part 6, Chapter 1, the* Kama Sutra

Courtesans were popular and widely used in India during this time. Courtesans were worldly women who conducted the business of being purveyors of the arts of love. This topic is extensively covered because they were expected to conduct their lives according to rules and regulations that protected society and ensured their profitability and success. They tended to be educated women and were the best lovers because of their extensive knowledge of the *Kama Sutra*. Details include who should be taken as a lover and who should not, which acts of love were appropriate and inappropriate, and the issues involved in taking a longtime lover.

PART 7: ON THE MEANS OF ATTRACTING OTHERS TO ONESELF

"When a person fails to obtain the object of his desires by any of the ways previously related, he should then have recourse to other ways of attracting others to himself."
—*Part 7, Chapter 1, Verses 1–2, the* Kama Sutra

Part 7 of the *Kama Sutra* covers occult practices, aphrodisiacs, sex toys, spells to draw lovers to you or away from you, and astrology for love. Potions and remedies for love-related problems are included, and impotency and libido are discussed, along with remedies to help mitigate problems. Plants, insects, herbs, spices, and other natural products of the time are suggested as solutions. Some of these "remedies" are very interesting indeed, and you can read more about them in chapter 9.

WHO TAUGHT THE *KAMA SUTRA*

"Man should study the Kama Sutra *and the arts and sciences subordinate thereto. Even young maids should study this* Kama Sutra *along with its arts and sciences before marriage, and after it they should continue to do so with the consent of their husbands."*
—*Part 1, Chapter 3, Verses 1–2, the* Kama Sutra

The *Kama Sutra* was written in short, rather poetic, verses—that way, it could be easily remembered by those who taught and learned it. Care was taken in who taught the young person the lessons, especially in the case of young women. Young men had more options as to how they learned the sexual arts than young women did at the time.

The perfect teacher of the *Kama Sutra* for a young girl was considered to be a faithful servant or an older sister. Other possible teachers might include an already married woman cousin, a trusted female companion who was married, or an aunt or even an experienced woman who had lost her husband and was celibate. Above all, the person was required to be trustworthy and dependable.

Thus, the *Kama Sutra* is the perfect text for teaching about sexuality, intimacy, and relationship skills. In our modern culture, there aren't many teachers of these vital subjects. Rather than honor our sexual nature, Western societies sometimes avoid the authentic topic or hide sexuality instead. High cultures in the past, like that of India, thought that sexuality was an important part of a healthy lifestyle. It was imperative not only to have sex but also to have good sex, even great sex!

Sex is considered a vehicle to higher consciousness in many Eastern religions, even today. In Taoism and Hindu Tantra, to name just two, sexuality is practiced in highly prescribed ways to enhance, build, sustain, and transmute the energy of orgasm. That energy is then used to flush the body with radiant energy, vision, clarity, health, and consciousness. Ritual lovemaking through ceremonial practices, with reverence to self and partner, becomes an alliance with spirit or god/goddess energy. This helps people become highly responsible for their own lives, and responsive to the lives of their loved ones, family, and community. It brings a reverence for nature and the honoring of the universal principles of life. When you identify with a goddess, you act like one! When you see your lover imbued with godlike energy, before your very eyes, he acts like a god!

"I never felt very good at lovemaking in my twenties and thirties. However, in my early forties I met a woman who was really into the Kama Sutra, *and my sex life took a 360-degree turn! I think everyone's sex life could be enriched from these ancient teachings and societies that honored sex like they did."*
–Aaron, 43

You can be your lover's teacher, and your lover can be yours. You are each other's gurus. Pay attention to the subtleties when looking at the pictures in this book. Note the quality and sentiment of the touching, the glancing eyes, the turn of the neck—it is all a kind of science. Study love. Know that the positions are one thing, but that the intention of love is the higher goal. Use each lesson, each position, and each variation much like those lovers from the past used the *Kama Sutra*—with a playful spirit, a sense of adventure, and the true knowledge of the divine in you and your lover.

"We practice Western Tantra, a set of practices that honor and enhance our sexual relationship. The ancient Kama Sutra fits well with Tantra in many ways. We have a kind of magical sex ritual we do where the ecstatic, hot energy gets wild and my lover almost always has multiple orgasms!"

—Brad, 33

2

The Preludes to Sexual Union

"How delicious an instrument is woman, when artfully played upon; how capable is she of producing the most exquisite harmonies, of executing the most complicated variations of love, and of giving the most divine of erotic pleasures."

—The Ananga Ranga

These wise words give voice to the notion that when we are present, loving, and giving to our partner, we receive the same back in generous amounts. Together we spiral upward, in ever-expanding pleasure. Every man and woman has his or her own preferences when it comes to sex, so the more you know about your own body, the better you'll know what rocks your world.

Dancing in the delicate play of your intimate sexual life, you will continue to discover the delicacies of your lover's body, mind, and soul. Knowing and learning how they love to be courted, embraced, spoken to, kissed, and made love to is the fine art of sexual loving. The nuances and subtle touches that each lover craves are waiting to be discovered, over and over again, in each of you. To play in this way, to learn to be your lover's best conspirator (con-spire = breathe together) in love is what the game is all about.

THE NATURE OF MEN AND WOMEN

The Taoists have a saying that goes something like this: "Women are made of the heavens. Their sexual energy comes from the heart and moves downward to their genitals. Men come from the earth. Their sexuality comes from their genitals and moves up to their heart." In other words, women need love and intimacy before they'll open their legs, and men need sex before they'll open their hearts. A generalization, to be sure, but it often holds true—hence the Venus and Mars analogy. Couples must work to bring the two realms together for the healing power of great sex!

Of course, there is much more egalitarianism now than in the days of the *Kama Sutra*. The forces of culture that require us to play one role or the other are diminishing in many aspects of our daily lives. No longer must we follow rules that say only the man should invite a woman out on a date. Women are empowered to be out in the world just as much as men. Women are also taking control of their pleasure and asking for what they want.

This greater equality doesn't diminish the need for both sexes to sometimes embody older, more traditional roles. Women love to be swept off their feet, and men love to be admired for their muscles and their brains. Telling a woman she is beautiful and hot is still as important as telling her she is brilliant. Men, contrary to what is assumed, love to be tender, caring, and compassionate, as well as being bold and displaying their sexual prowess. Under it all, you are your erotic, animal-like nature, and letting it show is sexy and modern, but also, as we will see, an age-old turn-on.

attention to you, if it happens in a natural and relaxed way. Don't try to fake it, though—it is easy to spot a person who is forcing a bubbly personality. Authenticity is a great aphrodisiac for the right person.

EMBRACING

All of the formal instruction on the "embrace" and other obscure details in the *Kama Sutra* seems odd to modern people. There are many pages on the minute details of how to embrace or hug, where to do it on the body, and when the appropriate times are during courtship, marriage, and in public. Because Vatsyayana prescribed such detailed directions, it tells us that the ancient Hindus paid great attention to the processes of seduction, arousal, and foreplay.

How do you embrace your lover? Are you usually overt and forceful, or tempting and playful, or maybe even shy or coy? Consider ways in which you might make your embracing more creative. Taking your lover by encircling her waist with your strong arms and bending her over for a kiss, like in the movies, might be startling and thrilling. Coming up behind your lover and surprising him with arms thrown around his neck while you lavish him with kisses might solicit a sultry response. Even just sitting on his lap, with your head on his shoulder while he wraps his engulfing arms around you, is deeply satisfying.

The next time you embrace your lover, run your hands up and down his torso and thighs to create a little new energy. Begin to seduce her by holding her tightly with one arm and softly caressing her cheek with your other. Stand behind him and cup his penis in your hand while the other hand erotically fondles his chest and neck. Come up

behind her while you are talking and stroke her upper arms as you breathe the fragrance of her hair. Let your hot, moist breath blow gently on her neck. Speak softly into her ear and then back off so she doesn't assume you're only trying to change the subject, though you may be! Think of some variations of your own, and then surprise the one you love!

KISSING

Ah, kissing . . . it's probably one of the most erotic and sensuous acts of love. Kissing comprises eight more of the sixty-four arts of love. From pecking to deep kissing, these acts are peaks of emotional, ecstatic lovemaking. Kissing can be entertaining all by itself or indulged in over and over during the heights of passion.

Kissing can take many forms. Although Vatsyayana doesn't offer any instruction in actual kissing, he does go into great detail about when a certain kind of kiss should be used and under what circumstances. The *Kama Sutra* describes the kinds of kisses to use with a maiden, a more experienced woman, a wife, and a courtesan. It also prescribes places on the body where kissing is to be done. Kissing was considered very intimate, and the sutras include judgments about areas of India where people didn't follow the rules set out by the *Kama Sutra*.

The *Kama Sutra* was designed to make lovemaking exquisite, from the very first moment until the last. In the case of a maiden or young wife, at her first time of making love, the sutras caution the man to go very gently with her, taking care not to frighten her by being too forward. As her confidence grows, it is suggested that an increase in pressure and aggression be employed to heighten arousal and passion.

Rule of Love

What would it be like to go back to "beginner's mind" and experience your first kiss all over again? See whether you can put yourself into that place. Be playful, but act a little shy. Try playing bashful, curious, or reluctant with your partner. Ask him to "teach" you how to kiss. Then change roles and enjoy the game again.

Can you imagine what your first lovemaking experience would have been like had you both had some training beforehand? To be treated tenderly, with care and sensitivity, might have made it a much more intimate and fulfilling event. Men and women's emotional states can so easily be enhanced by the simple attention to timing, appropriate actions, and tender caring. Hot, erotic sentiments can build once trust is established.

And from there, anything goes!

According to Vatsyayana, "The proper places for kissing are: the forehead, the eyes, the cheeks, the throat, the bosom, the breasts, the lips, and the interior of the mouth." Men and women both like to be kissed on the eyes, cheeks, and earlobes. Not only is it erotic, but teasing those areas of the face also represents the kinds of kisses you might have received as a child, so they are about love, too. Beyond those places, things get a little hotter! Long, luxurious kisses on the inner thighs, the torso, and the nape of the neck are very intense and erotic. You can prolong them to the point of teasing and making your lover cry out for more intensity by applying chocolate syrup or whipped cream to any area of the body.

DIFFERENT TYPES OF KAMA SUTRA KISSES

The *Kama Sutra* also specifically describes the various different types of kisses that one lover can impress upon another:

Nominal Kiss: When a girl only touches the mouth of her lover with her own, but does not herself do anything.

Throbbing Kiss: When a girl, setting aside her bashfulness a little, wishes to touch the lip that is pressed into her mouth, and with that object moves her lower lip, but not the upper one.

Touching Kiss: When a girl touches her lover's lip with her tongue, shuts her eyes, and places her hands on those of her lover.

"I used to just grab my girlfriend and kiss her hard because I wanted her to know how much I wanted her, but she's taught me to take it easy, and allow the passion to build. She always starts slowly, and by the time she's covered every part of me with kisses, my body is throbbing with desire."

—Ben, 35

"I used to think that French kissing was all there was to kissing. Then I met Patricia! It was so erotic and sensual the way she kissed me, and then I got really good at it. It just took someone to teach me that it was all about juicy, sensuous, and deliciously slow mouth play."

—Daniel, 36

The details of kissing demonstrate how ceremonial and restrictive the lessons can seem. The behavior seems ritualistic. First kisses can indeed be powerful, and staying present during one seems unlikely for anyone, let alone a maiden. You can imagine that this part goes by relatively fast before the heat of passion takes over and sweeps the lovers away. For fun you can try some of the kisses described in this section and see whether you can distinguish between them.

In addition to the nominal, throbbing, and touching kisses described above, other types of kisses include descriptions of turning one's head, pressing hard with the lips and face, bending the head toward the other, holding the chin of the beloved, and pinching the lower lip with the fingers before approaching the mouth. The more interesting discussion moves on to playing emotional games with the lover while kissing. Mock fighting and contests are encouraged, along with feigned crying, quarreling, and competition. Kissing is quite an art!

Kiss of the Upper Lip: When a man kisses the upper lip of a woman, while she kisses his lower lip. This kind of kiss has great power in Tantric lovemaking. It is said to activate the nadis, or "energy channels," in each of the lovers. It begins with gentle, and then more forceful, sucking of the lips.

Clasping Kiss: When either the man or the woman takes both the lips of the other between his or her own lips.

Fighting of the Tongue: When either the man or the woman touches the teeth, the tongue, and the palate of the other, with his or her tongue. We would call "fighting of the tongue" French kissing, though it has never actually been attributed to the French. It's curious that the *Kama Sutra* would call it "fighting." In reality, it is more like exploring, melding, and surrendering. It's often saved for the height of passion, when lovers naturally become uninhibited.

"I have a new boyfriend—we've been seeing each other for several weeks now. We spend hours kissing each other, and it's like a dance: we start so light and slow, so soft, and then add a little probing tongue. We just kiss and kiss for hours. It's great! We are just enjoying this time we call 'before,' making it last."

—Dee, 34

When you read sections of the complete *Kama Sutra*, you begin to realize that the interplay of teasing, coyness, conniving, and even deceptiveness is all expected in the game of love. Think up some new, clever ways to seduce your lover. Plan something new, and watch how he or she reacts.

The *Kama Sutra* also emphasizes that love acts should be reciprocal—"Whatever things may be done by one of the lovers to the other, the same should be returned by the other, i.e. if the woman kisses him, he should kiss her in return, if she strikes him, he should also strike her in return." Lovers will always do the thing that they want done to them. This can be counted on, so if you find yourself at a loss, observe your partner and copy what he does to you. Whether it's kissing, oral sex, mutual masturbation, or any number of sensual advances, keep your eyes open for hints—your lover will think you are the perfect lover, and you won't have to be a mind reader.

KISSING LESSONS

How do you kiss? How does your lover do it? Is there something you can learn about kissing? Many men and women complain that their lover doesn't know how to kiss very well, and that their kissing actually turns them off. Kissing is one of the most sensuous, erotic, and thrilling things couples can do together. It can be done just about anywhere. So, what's to keep you from being a great kisser?

Our mouths, lips, and tongues are alive with nerve endings. Voluptuous lips are one of the sexual stimuli that turn on both men and women. We wouldn't love eating nearly as much if we didn't like the texture of things in our mouths. Kissing has an erotic power over us, and the better you are at it the more you'll get kissed. The pleasure you can deliver and derive from kissing can be expanded to take on an importance of its own.

Lesson One: Wet your lips generously right now. Use your tongue and moisten them well. Put your lips together in an exaggerated pout. As you pout, rub the insides around on each other and feel the silkiness of your own inner lips.

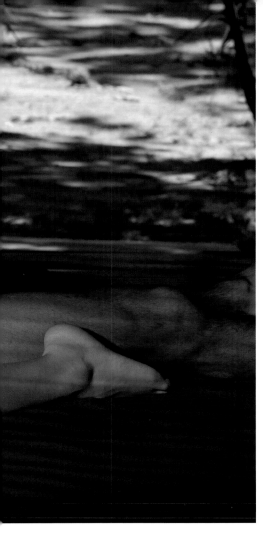

Imagine kissing that part of your mouth. Now, again exaggerating the pout, part your lips slightly so you can just suck in a little air through the opening. That is how your lips should feel when you are about to kiss someone: moist, juicy, voluptuous, open, and inviting.

Lesson Two: Kiss the back of your own hand as practice. You should leave a wet mark and make a small, seductive smack as you finish it. Slight suction can be felt when a full set of lips meets the skin. Attitude plays a big part in kissing, too. Are you being seductive and coy, or lustful and aggressive? Practice different attitudes while sucking and kissing various exotic fruits, such as a mango, peach, nectarine, or papaya. Peel the skin away and practice different styles of kissing while you're eating it. Nobody is going to see you, so go for it!

Lesson Three: Try recreating your first kissing experiences, as mentioned above. Tell your partner that you want to practice with her. Pretend you know nothing. Ask for pointers. You want to be a great kisser! Surrender some of the time. Be aggressive at other times. Dance back and forth with soft, slightly open, moist full lips.

Lesson Four: Don't introduce your tongue until after you've been kissing for a while. Wait until you and your lover yearn for it. When you do start tongue play, be playful. Tickle and tease. Run the tip of your tongue around the inside of your lover's lips. Give him a little tongue, then pull back and nibble at one lip. Run a finger erotically across her inner lips, and then leave it in the corner of your mouths while kissing. This gives a sense of urgency to the deeper kisses and adds extra sensuousness to the act.

Lesson Five: Sensuously introduce warm chocolate, juice, or liqueur into your lover's mouth before kissing. Share it back and forth. Lick the drips off of his lips in the most luscious way you can. Use your soft lips to kiss your lover's body all over. Ears are highly erogenous, so kiss, lick, nibble, suck, and bite an earlobe and breathe softly into the ear. You can create even more sensual pleasure if you slip down and kiss and bite the neck. In Tantric practice, a man's lower lip provides a direct channel to his sexual organ's excitement, so gently suck and kiss this area, too.

ORAL SEX

Oral sex was forbidden for chaste women to perform in many areas of ancient India. It was primarily the duty of eunuchs and courtesans, and it was always the man who received it.

The straightforward examples provided by the *Kama Sutra* don't go much beyond the very basics of oral sex, but they are a start from which you can explore. Oral sex is a very intimate and vulnerable experience. Very often a deep trust must be cultivated between partners in order for oral sex to be accepted in an open, relaxed manner. It is often one of the only ways women can achieve orgasm, and for men it is one of the very things they lust after and love. Oral sex is an art unto itself.

The *Kama Sutra* also suggests that striking, biting, scratching, and other provocative actions can be used during oral sex. You can read more about those sixty-four arts in chapter 8.

Using your hands all over your lover's body during oral sex, especially on her favorite erogenous zones, can send the receiver into an orgasmic explosion of pleasure.

THE EIGHT ORAL ARTS FOR MEN

While there are many other oral acts that you can create, the building of erotic energy is one of the most important "rules of love." Start your oral sex date out slowly and sensuously with one or two of the first steps noted above, and then add to the sensations by developing your own versions of the more intense steps, such as "sucking a mango fruit." It's all in the name of playful love games! The following descriptions will help you better understand what these set of eight oral arts entail:

Nominal Congress: "Nominal congress results when the man's erect phallus is placed between the lips, and holding it with the hand, it is moved about in the mouth." When you begin fellatio, it is very appropriate to begin on a soft penis. That way it can grow in your mouth. Most men like this very much. Use your hands to hold the penis upright as you begin to caress it with your lips.

Biting the Sides: "When, covering the end of the lingam with his fingers collected together like the bud of a plant or flower, the eunuch presses the sides of it with his lips, using his teeth also, it is called 'biting the sides.'" By holding the tip of the penis at the sides of the head you can steady it so that your lips and even your teeth can go down and back up the sides of the penis in a slow and seductive wave. Try a little light biting as you go, or save it for later, after you've taken a few more steps.

Pressing Outside: "Pressing outside is done when, upon being urged, the woman presses the tip of the phallus with her lips, as if drawing it in, and then lets it go." The woman presses her tongue against the tip of the penis. Try using this technique to tease your lover. You can feign interest when you start, then fool him into thinking he isn't going to get much, then surprise him by continuing to the next act.

Pressing Inside: "Pressing inside is done when the woman, on being entreated to do more, takes the phallus into her mouth as far as the man allows, presses its tip with her lips, and then ejects it. This is especially done when the lover wants oral congress more than the man." You've probably seen this done in porn movies. A woman can take the penis into her mouth multiple times, but at the end of each deep suck she lets the tip slip out of her mouth only to take it up again immediately and with more passion than the last time.

Kissing: "Kissing results when the woman grasps the phallus in her hands and kisses it as if she were kissing the man's lower lip." This can be done up and down the sides of the penis. Turn your head sideways as you kiss and lick up to the tip and down the sides of the shaft. You can nibble, too.

Rubbing: "Rubbing is done in the same way that kissing but is more extensive. The woman kisses the phallus on all sides with the tip of the tongue and the lips and strikes its end similarly." Hold onto your lover's penis with a flat palm and run your lips up and down the shaft rather firmly. Press your tongue against it both sideways and straight on. You can even use your teeth sparingly to softly bite the sides.

Sucking the Mango: "When, in the same way, she puts the half of it into her mouth, and forcibly kisses and sucks it, this is called 'sucking a mango fruit.'" This is the long, slow sensual act we all think of when we think "fellatio." When the man is at the height of his pleasure, slow this down considerably. Look him dreamily in the eyes while you are ravishing him with your lips.

Swallowing Up: "And lastly, when, with the consent of the man, the woman puts the whole lingam into her mouth, and presses it to the very end, as if she were going to swallow it up, it is called 'swallowing up.'" This final act is much like what you might call "deep throat." Go slowly if you try this technique. You can create a deeper feeling by using one of your hands on his penis to add to the effect of enclosing the penis all around.

"I love how outrageous my mouth feels when I'm giving my husband oral sex. His penis brushes by my upper palate area, on the outstroke, and I swear I'm going to orgasm when I do it really slowly. It's amazing, so I just focus on me. Selfish? Not really, because he seems to be enjoying it as much as I do."
—Laura, 37

Now that you have a complete list of the oral acts of giving fellatio, all that is left for you to do is to get creative. No order need be followed when giving oral sex to a man, although it is generally good to start slowly and erotically and build up the intensity. There are many tricks that can be used to make your mouth seem bigger than it is. You can wrap your thumb and forefinger around the base of his penis and squeeze as you move him in and out of your mouth. You can grasp the shaft with your hand or hands and stroke it, while with your lips and tongue you pleasure to only the bulging red crown of his penis. Pay special attention to that little V-shaped area on the underside, which is exquisitely sensitive. If he's uncircumcised, draw his foreskin up around the head and lick the part that peeks out.

Cup and pull his scrotum and balls while treating him to your warm, moist mouth during oral sex. You can massage his inner thighs and perineum and pull his pubic hair

Rule of Love

Cunnilingus is the term for giving pleasure to the female's genitals with the mouth and tongue. It is derived from the ancient words cunti and kunda: "womb of the Mother" or "womb of the universe." *Fellatio* is the term used for giving pleasure to the male's genitals with the mouth and tongue. Root words from the Latin include references to "swollen" and "sucking."

gently. Also, rub his heart area and fondle his nipples. Use both of your hands to open his thighs, then run your fingernails gently over his scrotum. You can stimulate another highly erotic area at the base of his penis, beneath his skin, by massaging firmly with your fingers. Use some lubricant or unscented massage oil all over his thighs and scrotum while you are ravishing him with your mouth. Try a bit of warm liquid in your mouth just before going down on him, or surprise him briefly with a small ice cube in your mouth! He'll be delighted at the effect.

Many men love to have their anal area massaged and fondled while receiving oral sex. See whether your guy would like to have you massage this area. (Some couples might choose to use a latex examination glove for this massage.) Use lots of lube, and first circle the anus with your finger until you feel it relax. Go slowly and make sure he is really turned on. Ask permission to enter him, and again go slowly, playfully teasing and opening him up while ravishing his penis with your mouth.

Although it is wonderful to recline and receive oral sex, sometimes the setting is right for the man to be standing or kneeling. It's a powerful position to be in and will often help a man who is having a bit of trouble with his erection. Have him kneel on the bed and sit on his heels or rise to a kneeling position. Kneel before him and fondle his balls while giving him fellatio. Bring him close to peaking, and then relax and go easy so he doesn't climax too quickly. Oral sex is a great way to practice waves of pleasure without ejaculating. It is one of the steps to ejaculation mastery.

THE ORAL ARTS FOR WOMEN

Some of the movements and actions that are described in the *Kama Sutra* for men can be applied to oral sex for women, too. A lighter touch is recommended, though, as the surface area of the clitoris is much smaller than the penis and much more sensitive.

Women orgasm much more consistently with clitoral stimulation than with vaginal stimulation, so you can think of the clitoris as her pleasure button.

In comparison to a man's genitals, which are fairly accessible because of their location on the front side of the body, the woman's can be a little elusive sometimes. A woman's vulva, including the outer and inner lips and the clitoris and clitoral hood, are relatively hidden. The clitoris has the largest concentration of nerve endings of any body part in either gender. It is so sensitive that simply the right pressure, place, and speed are required for orgasm. Stroke a little too fast or too hard and she'll shrink from your touch. Light, slow, broad stroking is good because usually it's only after gentle stimulation and arousal that she is ready for a firmer stroke.

The Art of Love

One of the most pleasurable and under-touched erogenous zones of a woman's body is her feet. Her lover can give her a taste of the sensuousness of fellatio by caressing, kissing, and then sucking her toes. Start with the baby toe and work your way to the big toe. Sometimes it's surprising how stimulating toe sucking can be!

It is really important that women pleasure themselves often, with their hands and with vibrators, so that they know what kinds of touch they like and the stimulation that makes them climax. If a woman doesn't know her own body, she isn't going to be able to experience orgasm with any consistency.

PERFECTING THE ART OF CUNNILINGUS

Here's a fun exercise for women that will expand your knowledge of your clitoral erogenous zone. This is a wonderful lesson that will help bring more passionate delight to your sexual adventures.

Start by lying down and relaxing. Warm a good-quality lubricant in your hand, and then generously slather some onto your vulva and clitoris. Now, starting very slowly and with a very light touch, begin to move around the sides of your clitoris with just the tip of one finger. You may want to gently pull back the clitoral hood with your other hand to free your clitoris.

Imagine a clock over your vulva, with noon at your pubic mound. As you are moving slowly around your clitoris, feeling the sensations as you go, notice where you feel the most delightfully sensitive. You might be surprised to know that about 80 percent of all

women are much more sensitive at about the two or three o'clock area, which is your upper left. Where are you most sensitive? Are you amazed that it is that exact?

Now that you know which area of your clitoris to focus your attention on, share this wonderful discovery with your partner! Show him what works for you, and include the locations you like, as well as the pressure and speed. It's fun to plan a date where the two of you show each other what turns you on when you self-love.

Then, when you get to oral sex, have your partner try different strokes, licks, gentle sucking, nibbling, humming, and soft blowing during cunnilingus. The usual position is for the man to lie between her legs, facing her while she's on her back. Another powerful position is as she lies on her back, the man kneels above her head to the side on which she is most sensitive on her clitoris. If it's the two o'clock spot, then he is over her left shoulder. This puts his tongue's stroking pressure directly on the best spot. It is also easier on the man's neck, especially if he is going to be there a while.

Another good position for cunnilingus is to have the man at a 90-degree angle to the woman. He then strokes her clitoris with his tongue from side to side and just a bit over the head of the clitoris, up over the shaft area. You can feel this area with your fingers to identify it first. He should be on the side that has the greatest sensitivity for her.

Begin your erotic oral sex date by kissing her inner thighs, stroking them lightly, maybe biting them gently or licking in long, generous sweeps of the tongue, and then move slowly inward, with focused attention. Take a more general kind of approach with your tongue strokes at first, but then use more specific flicks or circles, because women generally prefer to start slowly and build their passion as they go. Relaxation and trust are built this way, and so is her orgasmic response. As you begin to kiss her vulva, use your fingers

Rule of Love

You'll need to strengthen your tongue muscles to be great at oral sex. Get some tip-of-your-tongue exercise first by playing with a pea in a pod. You can also flick your tongue over and behind your front teeth, increasing pressure and speed. Focus your attention on the tip of your tongue to get the maximum benefit from your exercises.

"When my partner opens her legs to me and I see her beautiful self, I just want to taste and pleasure her until she orgasms. When that happens, I'm so hard that I just slide myself right into her and kiss her face until I climax myself, which isn't very long, usually!"

—Dave, 30

to tenderly separate the lips of her labia. You can kiss, suck, and lick the outer and inner labia, slowly working your way to the clitoral hood and the clitoris. Use longer, sweeping strokes of your tongue to begin with, and shorter strokes when you get near her clitoris.

Light, fast, flicking strokes made with the tip of your tongue are perfect. Focus on the spot where she is most sensitive. Women tend to like sustained, repetitive motions for a while and then a slight change of location and a slightly different stroke. Ask your partner what she likes at first, and then periodically ask her whether she likes what you are doing at the moment. You may want to experiment with changing positions a few times while you are performing cunnilingus. You'll soon learn and remember what her preferences are—though her preferences may change from time to time.

As she reaches the orgasmic zone, remind her to relax and breathe deeply into her belly. Women tend to hold their breath as they get close to orgasm, but this stops the action, so remind her to breathe! If she arches her back, that will give you more access to her clitoris. If she is tending to curl inward a little, you may be being a bit too firm in your touch. Back off a little and watch her response. Remember: the clitoris is very sensitive.

Rule of Love

During oral sex and intercourse, a woman will be more orgasmic if she remembers to relax. Try not to curl your body inward, because that causes the clitoris to hide under the clitoral hood and be less exposed to stimulation. You might use your fingers to hold the hood of your clitoris back to give greater access to your lover. It's stimulating and very erotic!

THE CROW POSITION OR "69"

The Crow Position may be the most classic *Kama Sutra* position of all! Known by every erotic explorer, the "69" position is versatile as well as mutually stimulating. To begin, either partner reclines in a comfortable position. In this version, he lies down and the woman lies on top of him, facing his feet.

As she approaches him, she can run her full breasts over his face, lingering there for a few kisses and sucks to her nipples. She then continues down toward his groin, brushing her breasts over his chest, stomach, thighs, and genitals. As she approaches his penis, she takes him slowly and sensually into her mouth and deeply inhales his mustiness. He, in turn, passionately nuzzles her vagina as she spreads her legs to either side of his head and lowers her hips to his lips.

The couple, through stroking and caressing, creates their special union by varying speed, depth, and movement. They can eventually roll over so that the man is on top, or they can lie on their sides for a while, heads resting on each other's lower thighs. They can also create a rocking motion, from head to toe, that adds friction to their eager sucks, licks, and kisses. The man should be gentle with his natural tendency to thrust his penis into her mouth, as he could choke her if he becomes too vigorous. Both partners should be conscious of shielding those tender parts from sharp teeth, too.

Both the man and the woman have their hands free to touch, caress, fondle, and massage each other's buttocks, breasts, and thighs. They can also add pleasure to the genitals by playing with the area around the perineum and anus. The man can titillate her vaginal opening and massage her G-spot. The woman can also suck on his scrotum and balls, pull on them gently, and grasp his penis with her hand and stroke it to pleasure more of him than just her mouth can hold.

3

Man Superior Positions

"Whatever is done by a man for giving pleasure to a woman is called the work of a man."

–Part 2, Chapter 8, Verse 4, the *Kama Sutra*

In the yin-yang, the female and male dance of love, it is the man who traditionally has the lead. The man is the aggressor, the leader, the virile, rough, and rugged guy who knows what he wants and goes after it. Though this is just another stereotype, most women do like to be "taken" by their man some of the time.

A man who is a great lover knows the arts of love and uses them to pleasure and please his lover. He is the leader in a seamless dance of love that uses sexual techniques skillfully, but not obviously. The man is the carrier of love when, with egoless grace, he offers himself up as a god might to his goddess, all for the sake of love and ecstasy.

MAN'S PART IN THE DANCE OF LOVE

The *Kama Sutra* describes the kind of actions the man should take during lovemaking to please the woman. Many of these love acts detailed below aren't common among modern lovers, so you may find this section of the *Kama Sutra* innovative and refreshing. Adventurous sex is important because it is the basis for finding out what creates the greatest pleasure and satisfaction for both partners. Is her G-spot being stimulated? Can he last? How is her clitoris involved? How can they have multiple peaks of pleasure without ending their lovemaking? How does the couple keep their lovemaking fresh?

The "love acts" to be performed by the man are examined here, and they amount to different ways of thrusting that can be used with almost any position. These techniques can add a new dimension every time you make love. Some will be easier in certain positions, while others will be more useful under different conditions. Create your own versions by exploring combinations of these moves.

The following love acts, taken from part 3, chapter 8, verses 12–20 of the *Kama Sutra*, should be performed by the man on the woman:

> **Moving Forward:** "When the organs are brought together properly and directly it is called 'moving the organ forward.'" This is the basic action of having the penis move in and out of the vagina. Adding specific thrusting patterns to this action greatly increases the arousal for both the man and the woman.

> **Friction or Churning:** "When the lingam is held with the hand, and turned all round in the yoni, it is called 'churning.'" Try this act sometime. Also use your hand on your own penis to massage the clitoris of the woman. Do this when you have a firm erection, and then rub the head of your penis on her clitoris. She'll love it.

> **Piercing:** "When the yoni is lowered, and the upper part of it is struck with the lingam, it is called 'piercing.'" This movement affects the G-spot area. When

the angle of penetration focuses the head of the penis up toward the top of the vagina it will rub against the G-spot, especially on the outstroke.

Rubbing: "When the same thing is done on the lower part of the yoni, it is called 'rubbing.'" The vagina doesn't have a lot of nerve endings in this area but deeper in the vagina, near the cervix, there is a region that many women find very pleasurable. This is the area stimulated by a deep downward thrust.

Pressing: "When the yoni is pressed by the lingam for a long time, it is called 'pressing.'" This action is about the depth of penetration and then holding the thrust while deeply inside of her. This movement can feel very good, especially if the man is getting too close to ejaculating and the woman is contracting her PC muscles while he is deep inside of her.

Giving a Blow: "When the lingam is slightly removed from the vagina, and then forcibly strikes it, it is called 'giving a blow.'" Be careful when you this move. If you strike the vagina or the penis and it's a little askew, you can hurt yourself. There is also the possibility of forcing air into the vaginal canal of the woman. This is dangerous, especially if the woman is pregnant.

The Blow of a Boar: "When only one part of the yoni is rubbed with the lingam, it is called the 'blow of a boar.'" If a woman knows her own vaginal area well, and recognizes what gives her pleasure, she can request her lover to focus his attention on that area of her anatomy. Some women love thrusting and stimulation on the area near their cervix. Other women like focused attention on their G-spot area. Whatever area is best for you, make sure you and your lover pay attention to those erogenous zones first.

The Blow of a Bull: "When both sides of the yoni are rubbed in this way, it is called the 'blow of a bull.' It is like the bull thrusting its horns from side to side." This technique sounds very erotic and can be used in some positions better than others. It implies a kind of swinging from side to side with a movement of the hips. Women-on-top positions are a good category in which to try this technique.

The Sporting of a Sparrow: "When the lingam is in the yoni, and moved up and down frequently, and without being taken out, it is called the 'sporting of a sparrow.' This takes place at the end of congress." This action often precedes ejaculation. The quickening of the movement means the man is close to orgasm and ejaculation. For a woman who is paying close attention, this movement is a good indication to slow things down if she doesn't want her lover to ejaculate. Paying attention to indicators like this can help train a man to last a long time.

Some of the descriptive actions above involve knowing where the nerve endings are on a woman's genitals, as well as what will turn her on. The "rubbing" strokes have to do with the positions of the penis inside the vagina; upper, lower, and side areas of the interior of the vagina have different qualities of feeling. Generally, rubbing the upper area touches the G-spot in the closest part of the interior. Striking the lower area stimulates the back end of the vagina near the deeper nerve bundles, which some women find very arousing.

"I go into a trance when my boyfriend is in a steady rhythm, but when he slows or stops his thrusting, I come out of it and look at him, knowing he is delaying his climax so we can make the sex last even longer."
—Tara, 32

The "pressing" action is when the man thrusts deeply into the vagina and stays there for long periods. This is a great time to squeeze and pump the PC muscles and lightly shift the hips, making subtle movements that keep the action intimate and erotic. The "sporting of the sparrow" involves the quickening that happens when the man, in particular, is very aroused and is getting closer to ejaculating. Then his movements speed up naturally, especially if the man is breathing fast and not paying attention. This is the time he can consciously slow down, breathe deeply, and spread the sexual energy throughout his body to experience the waves of ecstasy without coming. By doing these things he can easily train himself to last a very long time.

THE IMPORTANCE OF LONG LOVEMAKING

The study of new positions and techniques in lovemaking is practically impossible without a man who can maintain his erection without climaxing. It is imperative that he stay tuned in and maintain a full erection for the several positions you might want to try in an evening. This can be frustrating and hopeless unless his timing and ability to completely relax in high states of arousal are developed.

Learning to control and master male ejaculation is a fun and relatively easy undertaking. It involves playful, experiential learning in a solo setting and as a couple. If you practice at least three times a week, in just a few short weeks you'll both be very aware of the benefits.

The first things that you need to learn are in chapter 8, where you can learn about breathing for relaxation and excitement. You'll need to practice breathing on a daily basis, as many times as it occurs to you throughout the day. This is a very good thing, as it will extend your life span, among many other benefits.

Men and women both tend to start breathing faster and faster when they're exerting themselves, whether it is during sex or some other physical activity that increases the heart rate. Learning to slow your breath down and breathe deeply into your belly is imperative to good health and great sex. Once you're good at it, you won't have to pay much attention to ejaculation mastery because the actions will become somewhat automatic. That's when the sizzling passion really heats up!

CLASSIC POSITIONS WITH MAN ON TOP

Gazing down at your voluptuous lover as she lies before you, the slight perspiration glistening on her forehead, you prepare to plunge into her inviting warmth. She is yours, awaiting the gift of your manhood, to open her passions and pierce her heart. This is the picture the man has from his "on top" perspective. It is as inviting as it is thrilling. The dance of love begins.

Rule of Love

Men, relax your hips and the lower part of your torso while in the man-on-top positions. The more relaxed and supple you keep your body, the more fluid your thrusting will be. Your thrusting will be much more effective and erotic and the sexual energy in you will reach new and amazing heights.

BASIC MISSIONARY POSITION

With a passionate embrace, the man lays her down on the bed. She is flushed and ready for loving. She raises her knees and places her feet flat on the bed, allowing her lower back to rest on the bed and giving her the ability she will soon need to thrust, grind, and lift her hips in ecstasy. Her lover then lies down on top of her. Their lips meet for kissing.

The man enters her with his firm erection and the woman accommodates him by shifting her hips to make a perfect fit for the two of them. He supports himself on his hands and arms, and begins thrusting. The man moves his hips in rhythmic motion as his lover easily rises to meet his thrusts.

One of the great ways to stimulate the woman's clitoris during intercourse is for the man to move down to a hugging position, so that the lovers can put their arms around each other and move up and down, head to toe, to create friction and rubbing on her pubic bone and clitoris. This is one of the best ways to encourage a clitoral orgasm from a woman during intercourse.

Another interesting variation on this position is what is called the Coital Alignment Technique (C.A.T. position), and it is designed to stimulate the woman's clitoris during intercourse. It essentially begins as the missionary position, but then the man scoots up and rides high on her so that the base of his penis comes in contact with her clitoris. This places more friction from his pubic bone on her pubic bone. It also brings the top part of his shaft in direct contact with her clitoris. Then, as they move up and down, head to toe, the skin is pulled back and forth over her clitoris and his pubic bone rubs vigorously over her clitoral area. This technique works quite well and should be enjoyed whenever the Missionary Position is used. It will be very satisfying for both lovers.

> *"Because I'm so much bigger than she is, she often rides on top of me, but I love to be on top, too. When I'm on top, I support my weight on my arms and she can reach down and stroke her clitoris, which helps her orgasm multiple times."*
>
> *—Leo, 35*

TWINING POSITION

It's easy to move into this position from the Missionary Position. The woman reclines on her back as the man enters her from on top. She places one of her legs out straight alongside the man's legs and wraps her other leg over his hip and encircles his thigh. One leg may be better than the other to stimulate her G-spot just right. The subtle movements of her hips and the squeezing actions of her leg will move his penis over her G-spot in back-and-forth waves.

Her leg over his thigh locks on to him as they embrace. They can kiss easily in this position and the woman can use her "twined" leg to raise and lower her hips. They stay closely interlocked and can move up and down to rub her clitoris on his pubic bone or they can thrust together by moving their hips in unison in the in-and-out manner.

The woman's arms and hands are free in the Twining Position to rub, massage, and caress his back, hips, and possibly even his scrotum and testicles. She can reach a hand under his hips to fondle her clitoris, too. While leaning on his elbows the man can use his hands to caress her face and neck. This is a great position to kiss, nibble, suck, and even lovingly bite her neck, earlobes, and lips.

ALL-ENCOMPASSING POSITION

The All-Encompassing Position is comfortable and erotically stimulating, and the couple can move and maneuver well in it. Begin by having the woman lie on her back and draw her legs up, opening to welcome her partner. The man then enters her while kneeling. He opens his knees wide to grasp her buttocks between his thighs and sits on his lower legs. She wraps her legs around his lower back and upper buttocks, locking her feet over his back.

The man uses his arms to support his upper body, holding himself slightly away from her breasts. This will make his thrusting much more fluid and effective. With her legs over his hips, the woman is free to lift and lower her buttocks naturally to meet his deep thrusting and passionate moves. She can twist and turn her hips to create a "churning" effect in her vagina that will really turn both of them on. A pillow under the woman's buttocks will change the angle of penetration to aid in G-spot stroking.

The woman can stimulate her clitoris from this position, as well as fondle and caress her nipples and breasts. She can rise up slightly and suck his nipples and nuzzle her lips, nose, and face in his strong arms and chest. Tightening her legs up higher on his back will also change the angle of penetration and could make a difference in activating her G-spot. Changing that angle could help or hinder his ability to last, so pay attention to what works to achieve maximum pleasure!

CROSSING POSITION—MAN ON TOP

To begin, the woman lies on her back on the bed. The man then approaches her, kneels by her side, and straddles one of her legs with both of his. He embraces her leg with his as he enters her. The woman accommodates him by opening her outside leg, and pulling it up a bit as they find their fit together.

The angle of penetration will be slightly askew because of the arrangement of the legs in this position. This can be beneficial for the woman if she knows that her G-spot area is slightly to one side or the other. It can also be helpful for the man to gain control over his timing. This is because there may actually be less friction for his penis in this position, which isn't perfectly centered. Play with this position to discover what works for you and your partner.

This can be a great position for a man, and therefore his lover, when he has a larger than average penis. Straddling her leg provides a bit more space for the larger-sized man while thrusting, adding extra stimulation and friction for his pleasure. The higher the woman raises her outer leg, the more access he will have and the more his pubic bone will rub on her clitoris.

BEGINNER AND INTERMEDIATE *KAMA SUTRA* POSITIONS

Discover the attributes of these wonderful beginner to intermediate *Kama Sutra* positions and get creative with your lover!

VARIATION ON OPENING AND BLOSSOMING (PAGE 69)

BASIC MISSIONARY POSITION (PAGE 56)

CICADA AFFIXED TO A BRANCH (PAGE 145)

OPEN CHEST POSITION (PAGE 80)

BOUND IN HEAVEN (PAGE 79)

INVERTED POSITION (PAGE 78)

LION POSITION (PAGE 140)

BIRD POSITION (PAGE 135)

THE CRAB POSITION (PAGE 102)

DEER POSITION (PAGE 138)

SPOON POSITION (PAGE 97)

VARIATION ON THE ALL-ENCOMPASSING POSITION

In this creative variation on the All-Encompassing Position, the woman lies on her back as the man slowly and seductively straddles her. He widens his legs to support his hips, which gives him maximum leverage for thrusting. The man leans down and lies close to the woman as she wraps her legs and arms around him. She locks her legs at the ankles over his hips and buttocks and clings closely to his body.

The woman uses her legs to lift and grind her hips and make small thrusts to match his thrusts. She can move her feet and legs up further over his lower back to change the angle of penetration. She can cling to him even tighter as they rock and rub their bodies in ever-growing passion.

The man seductively pulls her hair, caresses her cheeks and forehead, and kisses her luscious lips. He nibbles at her neck and earlobes and sucks the tender parts of her upper arms. Being highly aroused, she scratches his back as she raises her hips to meet his. Her lust moves her to cling, thrust, scratch, and scream out in ecstasy as he relentlessly pleasures her without restraint.

WIDE-OPEN POSITION

The symmetry and beauty of this position is awe-inspiring. The Wide-Open Position is both visually inviting and erotically passionate. Begin this position by having the woman lie on her back as the man approaches her. He kneels close to her hips as he prepares to enter her. As he takes his first plunge, the woman bends her legs and pulls them as far up as she can toward her armpits. Her legs are open very wide.

Holding her knees as he begins to thrust, the man has a wide-open visual field to see his lustful woman. There is plenty of eye contact and both have their hands free to fondle and caress each other's skin. The woman can pull her lover's thighs and body closer, plunging him deeper into her. She can assist with the thrusting by holding him close.

This isn't a good position to foster clitoral rubbing by his penis or pubic bone, but it is a great position to allow either one to pleasure her clitoris manually. If he does the caressing, she can hold her legs back and open wide. If she is fondling her pleasure button, he can hold her legs open. The G-spot is also greatly stimulated in this position, especially if the woman holds her own legs back tightly, as it raises her pelvis and makes the angle of penetration more acute.

It's extremely erotic to watch her body from the Wide-Open Position. Her breasts will rhythmically bobble up and down as he hungrily thrusts into her. Without a pillow under her head, her body will undulate naturally under his touch, giving a sense of freedom and abandonment to the moment. She can fondle her own breasts and caress his body while he ravages her with passion.

ADVANCED AND ESOTERIC POSITIONS

Exotic, rare, and renowned in ancient times, the positions in this section are considered advanced because they are a bit more difficult and require very flexible bodies to execute the moves. Nevertheless, if they aren't too challenging for you, the rewards will be very satisfying, to say the least. Any position that has the woman's legs up high in the air, or near her chest, is going to be very stimulating for her G-spot. Her hips shift so that the upper area of his shaft and the head of his penis rub dramatically on this area inside the woman.

In Tantric practice, some of these positions are considered magical because of the intimacy and symbolic structure of the bodies they form. Descriptions like "liberation," "communion," and "karmic dissolution" are ascribed to some of these positions. Many couples discover that from time to time, they find themselves in a position that feels rather spiritual or magical. It is these enlightened feelings that led the ancient erotic explorers to write these very treatises on Love.

The Art of Love

Tantra is an ancient esoteric concept that means "to weave the world into existence." Many practices contributed to its teachings, but the most controversial and titillating of all was sex. Often this took the form of ritualized sexual events where many cultural taboos were broken, both for the sake of the ceremony and in order to transcend the earthly body and desires.

PACKED POSITION

The Packed Position may look difficult, but it is excellent for a woman who is relatively agile. It's a great position for G-spot stimulation, for any size penis, and for erotic, hot sex! Relaxed and waiting in delight, the woman lies on her back on the lovemaking bed. The man approaches her on his knees. He surrounds her voluptuous buttocks with his thighs and knees as he enters her.

The woman raises her legs into the air and brings them down, crosses them at the ankles, and places her feet upon the man's belly. She grasps his thighs and he reaches for her knees. They pull closer to each other, sending him deep inside of her. They use each other's bodies for traction and support for thrusting together.

As they rock and thrust, the man can use his hands on his lover's knees to maneuver her for greater pleasure. If he pushes them closer to her chest he will cause her pelvis to tilt up, putting more friction on her G-spot. He can establish a rhythm by leaning on her knees, and make quick flicks with his penis or deeper, plunging thrusts. The woman's crossed legs cause her vulva to close around his penis, thus creating even more thrill and excitement for both. He can rise up and down on his knees to shift the angle of penetration, and he can fondle and caress her breasts and even sensuously suck her toes.

LOTUS-LIKE POSITION

In the height of passion, the couple moves from the Packed Position to the Lotus-like Position. The woman crosses her legs, like a yogi in the lotus posture, and pulls her knees closer to her chest. Her lover leans further over her and moves deeply within her. Her feet move closer to his chest and higher up as he lustfully strokes her G-spot with the head of his swollen penis.

The more the man leans over, on top of his consort, the more her pelvis tilts upward, causing even more friction for both of them. The higher a woman's legs are toward her head, the greater the

angle of the penis and vagina in relationship to each other. This creates more pleasure for both the man and the woman. Achieving more pleasure is a double-edged sword, however. The man must be able to last with this level of stimulation.

A pillow under her bottom will lift her pelvis even more. Lifting the pelvis high in the air is good for men who have smaller penises. You'll get more bang for your buck with positions that have the woman's legs pressed up against her breasts or raised high over her head.

YAWNING POSITION

A wide-open pelvis and legs spread very wide is the posture taken by the woman in the Yawning Position. It might make her feel vulnerable, but she will reap the benefits because it is a great position for G-spot stimulation. To begin, the woman lies down on a comfortable surface and spreads her legs wide open, from the hips. She relaxes and opens her arms above her head for full surrender.

Her lover climbs between her legs and enters her. Although he is on top, he is also supporting himself with his knees and arms. The woman now opens her legs even wider and pulls her knees as far up toward her head as she can manage—the farther the better. This action tilts her pelvis upward and will result in his penis putting more pressure on her G-spot. The addition of a pillow under her buttocks tilts her pelvis even higher.

The man can hold her legs open, if she is really limber, or she can do it herself. She can reach under her buttocks to stroke, fondle, and pull his balls, or she can caress her own clitoris. She is so wide open that a man with a larger than average penis needs to be careful in this position. Shallow thrusting with an occasional deeper thrust is ideal, as long as he takes care not to plunge too deeply.

VARIATION ON YAWNING POSITION

This is a fantastic position for a G-spot massage! Don't be put off by this position—it isn't that difficult. You don't really have to draw your legs back onto your breasts as far as the very seductive photo shows to really enjoy the Variation on the Yawning Position. Placing a pillow under the woman's buttocks helps lift her legs and creates a better angle for penetration.

With lavish kisses and tender touching, the man assists his beauty in lying down on her back on a comfortable, spacious bed. Lightly touching her neck, breasts, and belly with only his fingertips as he approaches her, the man tips her pelvis upward and eases her legs back toward her head. He kneels over her and enters her.

The woman adjusts her legs and he supports himself with his hands as he moves over her, pressing his chest to her thighs. He can adjust his body to the level of her ability to stretch. Once in position, the woman can rotate her hips and use her hands to keep her lover close and to gain traction against his thrusting technique. She can hold her own legs, hold his thighs, reach under her own buttocks to cup his balls, or hug him closer and caress his arms.

Rule of Love

The angle of penetration is all-important for vaginal and G-spot orgasms to occur. A good technique to help you understand this is to make a circle with your left hand, connecting your index finger to your thumb (like the A-OK sign). Notice that your other fingers on this hand fan upward over the circle. Take your index finger of your other hand and poke it through the circle. Now, do this again, but aim your poking finger up toward the fanned fingers. If your fingers were her vagina, this would be the area of her G-spot, which you want to maximize contact with!

ONE LEG UP POSITION

This is another fantastic position for G-spot stimulation. It's a little easier on the hips of the woman, and she can rotate her legs to increase the intensity on one side of her vagina or the other, depending on what she likes. It's very erotic and wonderfully close for kissing, eye gazing, and watching your partner writhe in ecstasy. The One Leg Up Position is best when the height of passion is aroused beyond reason!

The woman lies down on her back and gazes adoringly at her man as he straddles her hips and buttocks with his knees. She raises one of her legs up to his shoulder and the other leg is suspended in the air, to the side of her body, to balance her. The man presses his body against the leg that is on his shoulder, and she holds him close for a deep, perfect fit.

The woman uses her leg on her lover's shoulder to maneuver, rock, and press against him for maximum pleasure. As he thrusts vigorously, she can work with his rhythm to achieve her own, matching and accompanying motions as they go. By gently swinging her outside leg, her pelvis will rock sideways, causing his swollen penis to brush back and forth over her G-spot. This is highly erotic and stimulating for both the woman and the man. They can fall into a rhythm that carries them to the outer limits of bliss.

The man can use one of his hands to caress her breasts and nipples or to press himself closer as he moves in and out of her. The woman can use her leg, the one on his shoulder, to twist and grind her hips for even more over-the-top sensational stimulation. Study the information on ejaculation mastery later in this chapter. You'll find it very handy for this position!

OPENING AND BLOSSOMING POSITION

The Opening and Blossoming Position is a natural progression from other positions covered in this chapter. In this variation, the man is upright and has more control over his lover's legs. It is a position for the heights of passionate lovemaking, and it can be a favorite for those who tend to get carried away by erotic energy. The woman needs to be relaxed, open, and willing to be taken in this manner. The man is in control.

The woman lies on her back and lifts her legs, while her lover straddles her hips with his thighs and knees. He boldly, yet lovingly, enters her as he lifts her straight legs in front of him. He uses his hands to balance himself as well as maneuver her legs. As he holds her legs together, he pushes them slightly away

from himself. His hands maneuver her legs, and therefore her pelvis, vagina, and G-spot, up and down and all around. A pillow may come in handy to lift her buttocks even more to meet his thrusting shaft.

The woman's hands are free to pull him closer for deeper penetration. She can massage his scrotum, her clitoris, or her breasts and nipples, while her lover skillfully manipulates her body for their pleasure. This position can be adapted for a standing position. The man stands by the bed while his lover is situated at the edge with her buttocks just slightly over the edge. That variation enables the man to have more control over the movements of his own body, and deepen his thrusting actions.

VARIATION ON OPENING AND BLOSSOMING

In the Variation on Opening and Blossoming Position, the woman straightens her legs out as the man leans into her legs more fully. Begin this position by laying the woman on her back on the bed. She then raises her legs straight up in the air as her lover approaches her thighs to enter her. He wraps his thighs around hers and maneuvers her hips to allow for the right angle of penetration.

As the man enters her, he brings her closer and guides her hips up and down for his pleasure. The woman can hold her own legs up to free her lover's hands for caressing her body. Her legs can remain in front of him equally, to either side of his head, or over one or both of his shoulders. She can also shift her legs to one side or the other to allow his penis to hit her G-spot just right.

The man can use his hands to press and release her legs, which will cause her to tighten and release around his penis. This action is very stimulating, so pace yourself or you might find that it will be impossible to last! Use a pillow under the woman's buttocks to lift her higher for more G-spot stimulation. Again, this position can be modified to a standing one. If the man stands at the edge of the bed all the same moves can be used to further enhance this erotic position.

INDRANI POSITION

Many of the previous positions discussed are very good for couples where the man's penis is fairly large and the woman's vagina is of a smaller size. Any position, including this one—the Indrani Position—that spreads the woman's vagina open rather widely, so that her lover has direct access for deep penetration, is in this category. The Indrani Position is named after the wife of the supreme god Indra, of early Vedic and Hindu culture.

To begin this position, the woman lies on her back with her knees pulled up to her breasts. The man then straddles her hips and thighs as she brings her lower legs over his upper thighs. He enters her and leans down on her knees. This presses him closely to her and lifts her pelvis, thus bringing her G-spot into closer proximity to the head of his penis. Every time he leans toward her, her

pelvis tilts upward even more. His rhythmic leaning and in-and-out thrusting will drive her absolutely wild!

In this position the man can be on his knees, but if he is limber enough to be up on his feet the action will really sizzle. In any position, the feet give extra maneuverability to the man's pelvis. He can rock on them and lift his body ever so slightly to add pacing and variation to any position. In this position notice that the man is on his feet and his upper thighs are resting on the woman's thighs, giving him a point on which to rotate and be supported. Her thighs can handle this, and the little bit of weight will hold her vagina open more. She is also able to get her fingers down to her clitoris to fondle and stimulate herself. A pillow under her buttocks will also help lift her pelvis to meet his ecstatic thrusting.

ORGASM ACCORDING TO MEN

The Masters and Johnson's sexological study in the 1950s—the first of its kind—detailed, among other things, the response cycle that men and women go through during sexual activity. The graph that resulted from the study illustrates how our sexual response cycle first increases during the arousal phase, levels off but stays high in the plateau phase, peaks during the orgasm phase, and then rapidly decreases after orgasm, during the resolution phase, often sending the man into dreamland shortly after climaxing.

Newer models of orgasm, both for men and for women, are putting a whole new spin on the energy and power behind the "big O." In these models, the plateau phase peaks, then subsides just a little, then new heights of pleasure plateau even higher, subside, and go higher, and the cycle continues much like the steps on a ladder. In the case of men, this "peaking" can end in orgasm with ejaculation when they decide to let it happen, at whichever rung of the ladder they choose. In the case of women, they can orgasm, build the energy again, and orgasm again, as many times as they want to fulfill their desire.

Orgasm and ejaculation don't necessarily occur together. They can be, and in fact are, independent events, although it doesn't feel that way to most men. There are techniques, which are quite simple to understand, that allow men to learn to separate the two and thereby last a much longer time and actually have multiple orgasms. There are many great books and DVDs on this subject, and men are highly encouraged to study this art of love. You'll find a brief explanation below but can also find more on the subject on many Web sites, such as www.tantra.com.

> *"I've been doing my PC muscle exercises for about two years now. I can't believe how great they make sex. My vagina is so tight I can feel everything my husband does inside of me. I can feel it when his penis starts to really swell and then I know I can let go so we orgasm together. I love that feeling!"*
>
> *—Kallie, 37*

THE PROCESSES OF ERECTION, LOVEMAKING, AND CLIMAX

A man's penis swells because of blood filling the spongy tissue of his penis when some physical, visual, or auditory stimulus arouses him sexually. It is prevented from flowing out again by valves in the veins activated by his arousal. Since the blood flows out again around the outside of the penis, cock rings can be used to prevent it from flowing back out too soon, so he can sustain his erection. These devices can be of great use for older men, for men who have illnesses that compromise their erectile function, or for the thrill of increased sensation.

As the penis swells, arousal continues to build and the man is able to engage in intercourse. As his pleasure increases, his breath tends to get faster and faster. Breathing patterns have a lot to do with his ability to last longer before coming. A man who can sustain long periods of lovemaking will notice that he has peaks of pleasure, valleys, and then peaks again, like the waves in the ocean. A skillful lover can be compared to a surfer riding a never-ending wave of bliss. This pattern can continue until the arousal is too great and/or the couple decides that it is time to climax.

Orgasm with ejaculation is usually genitally focused for men. If the man is healthy, his contractions are generally strong and rhythmic, and last for about eight to fourteen contractions. The resolution phase, as described by Masters and Johnson, usually comes very rapidly after a man ejaculates, and he feels sleepy and satisfied. Younger men can often recover quickly, achieve an erection, and make love again, but older men usually need more time, sometimes hours or days, to be able to become erect again.

EJACULATION MASTERY

It is relatively easy for a man to learn to control and master his ejaculation timing. By doing so he will be able to choose when he wants to ejaculate. This has the benefit of making loving last. His woman will also benefit, as long lovemaking gives her the time to orgasm, too. The practices are fun. When was homework ever like this!

Men, it is best to for you to start these practices solo. By doing so you'll achieve a better understanding of your arousal phase. Start by self-pleasuring in a relaxed, nonstressed environment when you have a bit of time. Using a scale of one to ten, self-pleasure to an arousal level of about seven or eight. Stop, breathe deeply into your belly, and relax completely. Let the energy subside a little. Then start again and stay relaxed. Have at least three peaks before you let go and climax.

Don't let the temptation to ejaculate get the better of you. Just a little self-restraint will really pay off! Practice this technique at least three times per week for two weeks. When you can consistently control your orgasm, go on to the next step.

The next step is to do this same practice with a partner. Let your lover stimulate you, and communicate using words and sounds to let her know at what level you are on the scale. This will be a bit more

4

Woman Superior Positions

"When a woman sees that her lover is fatigued by constant congress, without having his desire satisfied, she should, with his permission, lay him down upon his back, and give him assistance by acting his part. She may also do this to satisfy the curiosity of her lover, or her own desire of novelty."

−Part 2, Chapter 8, Verse 1, the *Kama Sutra*

FEMALE AS INITIATOR

There are many reasons why the female craves to be the initiator. A lustful woman, in modern times, has permission to take control of the lovemaking when she is aroused to do so. In the time of the *Kama Sutra*, the conditions in which she might show her passion were more restrained, yet according to the Tantric practices the female is considered the initiator. She is the temptress and represents the powerful feminine principle. Her Sanskrit name is Shakti, and the idea of feminine power is so pervasive that the term is actually the name given to the goddess, too.

CLASSIC POSITIONS, WOMAN ON TOP

These positions, so straightforwardly named, are the classic woman-on-top positions with which everyone is familiar. Although they seem so normal now, they were a little risqué in the days of the *Kama Sutra*. Since men are so visual, most men love these positions and their variations, because they can see the woman's breasts, stomach, smile, and expressions. It is a turn-on!

WOMAN ACTING THE PART OF THE MAN

Men appreciate change. They often feel as though they have to be in charge and responsible for the sex being "good." When the woman is on top, she can take greater control of the penetration angle, as well as the fondling of her breasts and clitoris, which allows the man to relax. This is also prime time for men to practice ejaculation mastery, which you read about in chapter 3.

Begin this position by having the man lie on his back. The woman straddles him and sits upright, her knees at his sides with her weight upon them. She slowly and seductively lowers herself down onto him. Her knees squeeze him tightly as she rides him up and down and forward and backward. She can swing her hips and grind them in circles to vastly improve the arousal and buildup of sexual energy. The woman controls the depth of penetration so that she can position his penis just right for her G-spot.

"I love to be 'on top' when my husband and I have sex. It's so much easier for me to stimulate my G-spot because I know exactly where that little spot is. Also, I love to use my vibrator to stimulate my clitoris, so that way I have both clitoral and G-spot orgasms—making me one happy, sexually gratified woman!
—Erin, 35

BOUND IN HEAVEN

Another natural inclination of a very turned-on woman is to reach forward and "pin" her lover to the bed. This is the Bound in Heaven Position. The man lies on his back and the woman straddles him with her knees on the bed, wrapped around his torso. She reaches forward and pins his shoulders or arms to the bed with her hands as she moves backward and forward, up and down on his penis. Her stomach should be low so that her clitoris rubs on his pubic bone as she moves over him.

In this way she supports some of her weight on her arms, relieving her knees and legs of some of the effort of her movement, and she gains traction to move even more wildly. One of the great benefits of this position is that the man has full access to her breasts. He can suck them, and she can sweep them to and fro over his face. A fantasy fulfilled!

> "I love pinning my husband's arms down, and then laying my cheek on his warm chest and hearing his heart beat. He wraps me in his arms and I could just stay that way forever, except that it feels so good to rock him inside me that I go back and forth between the two."
> —Anna, 38

A wonderful variety of thrusting patterns are easy in this position, too. With woman-on-top positions, she is in control of her ecstasy and therefore can position herself for maximum G-spot pleasure. While she bends forward to give him access to her breasts for sucking, her hips will naturally move upward, which puts his penis and her G-spot in better contact. She can dip deeply and then pull up while she feels the head of his swelling penis brush exquisitely past her G-spot, again and again!

OPEN CHEST POSITION

The Open Chest Position is very visual and extremely erotic. It is a prime G-spot position because his penis will rub against the upper inside of her vagina, right in the area of the G-spot. She can rise up slowly and deliberately to maximize both her and his pleasure!

To begin this position, the man lies on his back and the woman straddles him on her knees. Once he is inside her, she bends backward and supports herself with her hands on his knees or on the bed, opening her chest and breathing deeply.

Her breasts reach for the sky as her lover's hands grip her waist and assist her in her movements. The man can help her rise and fall on him by holding onto her thighs and using his hands to lift her up and down. He can pull her forward and backward over his erect penis, and she can grind her hips or make short, quick thrusts in rapid succession to increase their pleasure.

The Open Chest Position is perfect for accessing her clitoris. If he is gentle and slow he can use both of his thumbs to surround her clitoris and massage the labia right around it. Using some lubricant, he can pull her clitoral hood up with two fingers and use the other hand to massage and stimulate her clitoris as she rides him to ecstasy.

COMPASS POSITION

The Compass Position is a variation on the Open Chest Position. It begins in much the same way, by having the woman straddle her lover, who lies on his back. On her knees she allows him to enter her. As in the Open Chest Position described above, she leans all the way back until she comes to rest on the man's legs, with her head between them. He can assist her by clasping her hands and lowering her slowly.

Though this is a woman-on-top position, she isn't in control. The man must use his hands to move her back and forth over his shaft. He grips her at her hips or thighs to orchestrate the movements. In this position his penis is bent somewhat toward his feet, and because she is leaning so far back, her G-spot and the head of his penis get a lot of stimulation. Simple thrusting patterns add variation to the back-and-forth action, but control is important so he doesn't pop out on an outstroke!

He can slow the action down and use his hands to massage her thighs and stomach. He can also use his thumbs or fingers to stimulate her clitoris very easily in this position. Pressing firmly down on her pubic bone, just above her pubic hair, will further stimulate her G-spot while he is doing shallow thrusting.

Rule of Love

Stay in close communication in the Open Chest Position because if she is bumping and grinding in passionate abandon, while the man rubs and squeezes her clitoris, it is vulnerable to too much pressure and friction. This can cause her to be irritated and turn her pleasure into pain. Men, watch her movements closely and be ready to adjust accordingly.

STEERING THE CART

This position, Steering the Cart, starts with the man lying down on his back with a large pillow under his upper body and head. She places a medium-size pillow between his slightly spread legs and a larger one just beyond that one. The woman then straddles and inserts him into her. Instead of sitting on her knees, as in the previous positions, she stretches her legs out and to either side of her lover's torso, and sits fully on top of him.

The man assists her by holding her hands as she lowers her body back onto the pillows. She should be propped up so she can see him clearly. He rises on his elbows and uses her outstretched legs as though they were handles on a cart or wheelbarrow to move her over him. If he moves her legs back and forth, alternating one and then the other, it will cause his penis to sweep across her G-spot area in a most titillating way. The swelling head of his penis will get a lot of friction in this position, so he should time himself and vary the motion to make it last. This variation will tease her into a convulsive orgasm.

Rule of Love

A word of caution: Both the Compass Position and the Steering the Cart Position create an extreme angle of penetration for the man's penis; be careful not to make any rapid movements or sideways turns so as not to hurt that precious love muscle.

TRAVELER'S POSITION

The Traveler's Position has the woman straddling her lover, much as in the classic Woman Acting the Part of the Man Position, but turned around so she faces his feet. He lies down on his back to begin. She straddles him and inserts his erect penis inside of her as she bends slightly forward, flashing her buttocks and vulva for his eyes only.

The woman rides him with up and down motions. The man can use his hands and arms to help her move and set the rhythm of thrusting. If he has a pillow behind him, he can sit up a bit and exquisitely massage and fondle her breasts.

With the woman's hands free in this position, she also can stimulate her breasts and nipples and easily reach her clitoris. She can also surprise her partner by fondling his scrotum and the sensitive base of his penis. A slight pull on his balls will help him last longer, too.

The man can place his hands at the base of her spine to push her hips and buttocks gently forward, to add friction and change the motion. She will spring back on her own, so he can get a dance going by simply pushing softly to a rhythm. This movement will also stimulate her G-spot.

TANDEM TRAVELERS

This is an interesting position that has the potential for some hot G-spot connection. Start by getting into the Traveler's Position previously discussed (the man lies down and the woman straddles him, but is turned around so she faces his feet). Once you've enjoyed each other with a little rambunctious play this way, the man sits upright and the woman moves down and adjusts herself to create space for both of them. She can lean forward slightly or more fully to allow for different angles of penetration.

Being on her knees, at either side of his hips, creates the spring action for her to move up and down on his erect penis. As the initiator, the woman has freedom in this position to set the pace and depth of the thrusting. She can lean far forward to change the location of his penis on her G-spot or to shift the pressure on her knees a bit.

This is also a fantastic position for her to receive a massage. The man can either massage her back and buttocks or caress her exquisite breasts, neck, stomach, and thighs. He can stimulate her clitoris and she can play with his scrotum, sensuously pulling his pubic hairs and stroking the firm base of his penis, even circling it with her fingers with a firm stroke.

TAKING CONTROL— ADVANCED POSITIONS

When the woman plays the part of the man and her erotic and passionate nature begins to take over, she will have a mind of her own. A woman in this state of mind is the most exciting and luscious lover. To take full advantage of the situation, her partner needs only to let her lead and keep up with her movements, inclinations, and wild abandonment.

CROSSING POSITION—WOMAN ON TOP

Rolling and Tumbling might be even a better name for this position! There is a lot of freedom of movement in the Crossing Position. This version is with the woman on top. Start by having the man lie flat on his back. The woman then straddles him by putting one of her legs between his and keeping the other one to the outside of his body, so their legs alternate.

The couple holds each other close as he inserts his penis into her vagina. Wiggling and adjusting, they wrap their legs around each other and use their legs and arms to help maneuver their movements. Both of them have the freedom to move their hips by gently thrusting together. They can both squeeze and release their PC muscles, too, for even more delight.

The woman can adjust from which side she straddles him for her own pleasure. She'll know the side she prefers if she is familiar with the position of her G-spot. The two of them can establish a forward-and-back, head-to-toe rhythm that will pleasure her clitoris. Their pubic areas will also become aroused from this very close rubbing.

It is very easy to make this position into more of a playful sexual dance by first moving back and forth with her on top, and then changing positions with him on top. Rolling and tumbling, they can flip over and reverse the action any time they want. Make sure she experiments by trying this position several different ways: with her right leg to the outside, and then with her left leg to the outside. It could make a big difference to her pleasure.

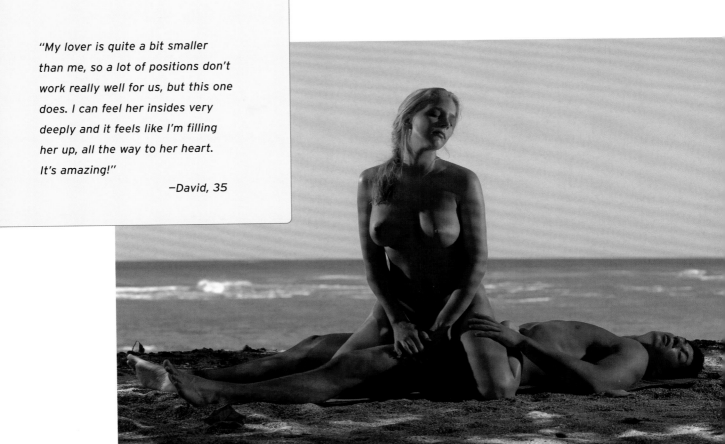

"My lover is quite a bit smaller than me, so a lot of positions don't work really well for us, but this one does. I can feel her insides very deeply and it feels like I'm filling her up, all the way to her heart. It's amazing!"

—David, 35

BUMBLEBEE SIPPING NECTAR

Many classic ancient texts depict positions with drawings that portray the woman as quite a bit smaller than the man. Many men who studied the arts of love had multiple wives—with many of these wives being much younger, and therefore generally smaller. Bumblebee Sipping Nectar is one of the positions that suits a larger man and a smaller woman. The man must be comfortable, lying on his back, and the woman should tease and stimulate him until he is erect.

The woman gently climbs on top of him, positioning herself on her knees with her weight on top of his legs, and then lowers herself onto him. Firm pillows around his hips and between his legs will help support the woman as she moves over him.

The woman can move her body to any point around a complete circle to position herself at the best angle for her pleasure. She can move up and down on him because of the spring in her legs in this position. Short, quick flicks of her hips, in a rhythmic beat, will excite both of them. If she has strong PC muscles, she can suck his penis in deeper and release and hold it for added intensity.

ALTERNATING FEET

This is a hot position to get the juices flowing. To begin, the man lies on the bed as the woman assumes her position by straddling and kneeling over him. She rubs her breasts over his chest and might kiss or nuzzle his ear to further arouse him because he needs to be very turned on and erect before he penetrates her.

Bringing one of her feet up, while the other leg stays kneeling, she plants her foot next to his hip. With her hand that is on the same side as her planted foot, she then grabs his hip or buttock and proceeds to take him for both her and his pleasure! This is a very active position for the woman, and good to use when she is feeling particularly lustful.

The woman can lift his hip and bring it toward her and rock him easily from this position. It doesn't take much strength. She can also tilt his hip to position the head of his penis more accurately for her G-spot. She can shift sides often or stay on the side that gives her the most pleasure.

The man has full access to her erect nipples and swollen clitoris for fondling. He can tenderly caress her face, neck, and arms as he tells her how sexy she looks and how good he feels. The woman can also reach under her leg that is still up to caress his scrotum and penis, stroking the shaft when it emerges from her.

SOARING AND FLUTTERING BUTTERFLY

This position is like one from a courtesan's secret diary. The Soaring and Fluttering Butterfly derives its name from its resemblance to a butterfly, with wings fluttering, hovering over a delectable flower. It requires strong legs on the part of the woman, and on the man's part, a willingness to let her take control. He is in for a ride, and he'd better relax or he isn't going to last very long.

Lying straight out on the bed, the man relaxes as his woman starts at his toes and, getting down low, slowly works her way up to her position by swinging and rubbing her breasts up his thighs, pausing at his penis. Arriving at his chest, she straddles him, after a long kiss, and gets up on to her two feet. He guides himself into her and she proceeds to move up and down on his penis.

The woman uses her legs to raise and lower her body over him. He can grip her buttocks with his hands and help her with the movements while she holds herself up with her hands on his chest. If she's practiced with her PC muscles, she should use them on the upstroke. This movement tugs at his frenulum, the area where the head of the penis meets the shaft, causing him much pleasure. It also causes more friction and pleasure for her as his head moves past her G-spot.

This position can get very fun and interesting when she employs a variety of thrusting techniques, like nine shallow and one deep, then eight shallow and two deep, then seven shallow and three deep, and so on until the end of the sequence, then reverse and go in the other direction with all shallow thrusts. It's also quite easy for the woman to "walk" or waddle right up to his face for some juicy oral sex. This is a very versatile position!

ORGASM ACCORDING TO WOMEN

Women are multifaceted in their pleasure, as in all things. They love soft, nurturing sensuality and even sexual activity that doesn't result in orgasm. They love the slow, delicious ride that lovemaking is when it is tender intimacy and soft caressing, and also sex that is animal-like—wild, hot, fast, loud—it all works for women. They just can't get enough of the most erotic pleasure!

A woman is capable of several kinds of orgasms that vary in duration, point or points of origination, strength, number, extent, changes in consciousness, and intensity. Her orgasms can feel brief, expansive, deep, short, extended, mild, earthshaking, odd—and any of a great variety of adjectives that might be ascribed to them. Strong ones can come when least expected, or they can turn out to be little "blips" after a long effort and great expectation. Even the most seasoned lovers can be surprised.

For many women, orgasm is elusive. They struggle to get to it, only to have it fall away, rise again, then fall away again, and leave them frustrated and doubting. If it eludes them altogether they can feel "broken." Most women can learn to have orgasms, but they must believe that it is possible for them. Because we lack mentors in sexuality, using books, the Internet, and educational DVDs is an excellent way to get the mind turned on to orgasm. Often, being shown that it is possible and how other women orgasm will make it attainable at last.

CLITORAL ORGASMS

Let's look at a few different kinds of orgasm. The clitoral orgasm is by far the most common type. It is generally very genitally focused, meaning it is mostly felt only in the immediate clitoral location. A clitoral orgasm is usually fairly intense because the clitoris has by far the largest number of nerve endings of any part of the body. A clitoral orgasm produces rhythmic contractions of the pelvis and clitoral muscle structure that often last from eight to twenty contractions, depending on the level of turn-on and the duration of lovemaking leading up to the orgasm.

Some women can have multiple, back-to-back clitoral orgasms, but the majority of women usually don't. This is because the clitoral tissue and the nerve bundle that serves the clitoris becomes too sensitive for touch after an orgasm. It is perfectly normal, as it is with most men, to have a refractory period before stimulation can start again that could lead to a second, third, or fourth orgasm.

VAGINAL OR G-SPOT ORGASMS

Most of the vagina isn't very sensitive to pressure or touch, but there are a few places inside the vagina that have nerve endings that contribute to orgasm. One of these locations is deep inside, behind the cervix, on the upper part of the rear wall of the vagina. The other location is the area of the G-spot, about 1½ inches into the vagina, on the upper wall, just behind the pubic bone.

You can find the G-spot area by inserting a finger into your vagina while you are kneeling on the floor. Slip your lubricated finger in slowly with the pad of your finger facing upward in the "come hither" motion, while feeling for a ridge-like area that is bumpy to the touch. If you miss it and your finger goes into a deep pocket, on the top of your vagina, you've gone too far. Pull your finger out slowly until you do feel the bumpy tissue. Then press in this area. It should feel sensitive to your touch, different from the flesh around it. Press firmly—the G-spot can take a lot of pressure.

Orgasm Helpers for Women

- Learn to breathe into your belly.
- Practice deep relaxation.
- Know your body and self-pleasure often.
- Ask your lover for what you like.
- Take good care of your health.
- Do your Kegel exercises regularly.
- Take high-quality fish-oil supplements.
- Drink generous amounts of water daily.

It helps tremendously if you are turned on already, maybe by clitoral stimulation, because the G-spot becomes engorged until you have an orgasm. The blood that fills the clitoral sponge also fills the area of the G-spot. The clitoris is much larger than what you can see. Its shaft goes under the skin and divides into two "legs." These legs carry the nerve fibers and wrap around the G-spot's spongy tissue, so the two are tied together in arousal.

G-spot orgasms may be felt throughout the whole body, compared to being genitally focused as clitoral orgasms are. They can be softer or fiercer, depending on the woman's state of mind and body. The potential for multiple orgasms is also greater because the nerves for G-spot orgasms have a different refractory period than that of the large bundle of nerves that cause clitoral orgasm, and the G-spot can take stimulation longer and more intensely than the clitoris can.

You can usually count on clitoral orgasms through oral or manual stimulation, but learning to have G-spot orgasms can be good if you like wild, passionate intercourse with your hands free to hold on, pull his hair, or stimulate other erogenous zones.

BLENDED ORGASMS

When you really want to go for it, blend your orgasms by stimulating your clitoris and your G-spot. This can be done by combining techniques to arouse both areas, such as oral sex with fingers stimulating the G-spot; oral sex and a good G-spot toy; manual clitoral stimulation and a sex toy; intercourse in a good G-spot-friendly position with manual clitoral stimulation; or a sex toy that does it all.

"Sometimes it seems I'm not going to orgasm with intercourse alone, so my husband gets out this little soft vibrator and puts it on my clitoris. It also vibrates his penis as he strokes in and out, which he likes. By really clenching him with my PC muscles I can have an orgasm inside and out—and so can he—so all parties are sexually satisfied!"

–Ruth, 36

Generally you begin by stimulating the clitoris to an arousal point of about seven on a scale of ten. Then add some vaginal penetration that targets the G-spot. Balance the energy, thrill, and attention between each place as your passion increases. Some women love anal stimulation, and this would be a great place to add a bit of play and stimulation around the exterior of the anus. You may even want to replace the G-spot stroking with the equivalent kind of strokes in the anal cavity. Keep it clean, though—don't go back and forth with a toy, finger, or penis without a thorough washing in between.

Blended orgasms can be very powerful. Remember to breathe deeply and relax. Make sure that you are having fun and being playful or this will look like hard work to you and your partner. It's all about play, so keep it fun and adventurous.

MORE ORGASMS—HALLELUJAH!

The good news is that more women are becoming orgasmic. As a society, we are much more talkative about sexuality and orgasms today than ever before. Magazines, erotic self-help books and programs, television shows, workshops, DVDs, and more all give us permission to learn and talk about sex and orgasms. The variety and availability of many different types of vibrators for self-stimulation is amazing. Find out what you like with long sessions of self-loving. Learn how your body works, and then you can guide your partner to greater mutual pleasure.

FEMALE EJACULATION

In the Sanskrit language, female ejaculate is called *Amrita*, or "the nectar of the goddess." It is considered holy, and Tantra places great importance on absorbing the female fluids during sexual intercourse as an elixir of youthfulness.

Many women ejaculate. Until recently there wasn't much information about female ejaculation, and the women doing it were naturally embarrassed by it because it's sometimes copious and can be mistaken for involuntary urination. Fortunately, times have changed and today not only is it accepted, but it is actively courted. It seems, when it comes to pleasure, that there are always intrepid explorers who want to be on the cutting edge of the latest knowledge.

Empty your bladder completely before you make love, as many women feel that when they are about to climax and are "letting go," they are going to urinate, although this isn't usually the case. Take a towel to bed with you and place it under your hips, just to make you feel more secure. Though typically the ejaculate is only about a teaspoon of liquid, some women produce much more than this.

Deep breathing, relaxation, trusting your lover, and knowing your G-spot will help you learn to ejaculate. It also helps to make deep moaning sounds, starting from the abdomen and pushing out with your PC muscles (much like birthing a baby if you've done this) just at the moment of orgasm.

Most women can ejaculate, but they just need to know they can and give themselves permission to do so. Their partners need to understand that female ejaculation is a sign of deep pleasure and that they can participate, too, especially with masterful stimulation of her G-spot. It's an exquisite feeling and most men get very turned on by it, once they understand what is happening and how pleasurable it is for the woman.

5

Lying and Standing Positions

"When a man and a woman enjoy their life in this way, with due shyness, modesty, and mutual consent, their love does not fade, even after a lapse of one hundred years, which is considered the normal life span of a man. Just as food, even when it is excellent, if repeatedly eaten day after day, loses its charm, so it is with Love."

–Part 2, Chapter 5, Verse 43, the *Kama Sutra*

To keep your relationship fresh, you've got to explore the mysteries of love, sex, and intimacy. There are sexual positions for all kinds of occasions and conditions that can add variety and spice to your lovemaking. Whether you've got all the time in the world or you've just decided to have a quickie in the elevator of your apartment building, it's important to have a large repertoire so sex never gets boring. Relaxing or arousing, the positions that follow are great for larger penises, for G-spot stimulation, and for prolonging erections.

LYING DOWN POSITIONS

The lying down positions serve several purposes for lovers. The positions categorized as "spooning" are generally restful, though this doesn't always have to be the case, as you'll see later. All of the positions below bring the couple into very close proximity with one another, creating a lot of bodily contact. Positions that involve the legs being relatively straight can be extraordinary for couples where the man has an overly large penis and for a woman who knows the power of her PC muscles!

"Sometimes my boyfriend wakes me in the night by slipping himself into my vagina from behind. I wiggle a little to let him in and we have sweet sex in that in-between, dreamy place, before drifting off to sleep again."

—Cheryl, 30

SPOON POSITION

The Spoon Position is often thought of as a cuddling posture. It can be considered a comforting, affectionate hug, or it can be used as a sex position. Usually the woman lies down in front of the man and he wraps his arm around her waist or higher up her chest so he can fondle her breasts and nipples. He can even reach her clitoris for that extra special caressing. She can rest her head on his forearm, and he can embrace her tightly from behind. The Spoon Position can be reversed, with the woman behind, if it is just to be used as a form of cuddling. It's very nurturing and enduring, and many couples like to fall asleep like this after their hot, erotic lovemaking is over.

The lovers lie on their sides with her back to his chest. It is common in Indian practice to have the woman on her left side, so if that feels right to you, then both of you can lie on your left sides. Snuggle up as you pull each other closer

for a tighter fit. She bends her legs so that he can enter her from behind. His hand can be between her breasts, on her heart, or holding her close to him.

Small movements, and a restful attitude, make this a great position for pregnancy, at any stage. The Spoon Position is good for when you are relatively tired or simply want to rest and cool down your passion before starting up again. It is a very nurturing way to relax.

Turn up the heat by having the woman bend forward, moving her head closer to her toes. This adjustment changes the angle of penetration and causes his penis to stroke her G-spot better. She can even reach between her legs to gently pull on his scrotum and caress his perineum. This is very erotic for him and can get him extremely aroused. It may also be stimulating for the woman to lift her top leg a bit for better contact on her G-spot and to reach his scrotum.

CLASPING POSITION

In the Clasping Position, both the man and the woman lie facing each other, with the woman preferably lying on her left side. Both of your bodies are straight and each of you has one free arm with which to caress.

The woman will briefly lift her top leg so that he can enter her. Once in, she lowers her leg and they pull each other even closer. She holds his penis inside of her and uses her thighs to tighten around it as they gently rock their hips and softly undulate to add friction to her hold. His hand can be grasping her buttocks, holding her closer and feeling her luscious skin and round, firm flesh under his fingertips.

Kissing, eye gazing, and breathing together in rhythm add to the thrill of this position. This is a good position for a man who has a smaller penis, especially if the woman has a larger vaginal canal. Tease her buttocks crack with a finger, or add massage oil to your fingertips for a slippery and sensual massage, or simply breathe, holding each other and kissing deeply while thrusting.

"I don't mind that my husband is smaller—we still have great lovemaking. When we both lie together on our sides, and I hold him inside of me, using my thighs to tighten around him, the gentle rocking and friction drive him wild, and it's a comfortable position for me to feel pleasure as well!"

–Michelle, 37

PRESSING POSITION

The next few positions are straight-legged positions. The first is the classic Pressing Position. The woman lies flat on her back with her legs straight out in front of her. The man lies on top of her and she separates her legs a bit so he can enter her. He then rises up a bit, supporting his weight on his arms, to allow her to close her legs by bringing them together, under him.

In all the Pressing Positions, the woman can squeeze his penis with her thighs as he moves in and out of her. They can vary this position by pumping their PC muscles in rhythm with each other, or she can pump hers alone. If he is very large, a combination of these friction-enhancing moves can really stimulate his shaft and her clitoris. For more clitoral arousal, rubbing bodies up and down, head to toe, is recommended.

This is a very close position. If the man is physically much larger than the woman, he may be too heavy to lie on top. In that case, they can use the Reverse Pressing Position, in which the woman is on top; this is discussed below.

REVERSE PRESSING POSITION

The woman is on top in this variation. The man lies down flat on a bed or soft mat. He separates his legs so that she can position her legs between them as she lowers herself face down on top of him, taking him inside her. A smaller woman can arrange herself between his thighs, but he should keep his legs fairly straight and together once he has entered her.

On a platform that has a sturdy end board or even a wall, he can push rhythmically on the wall with his feet to aid in the friction and rubbing on her clitoris and his shaft. This movement can quickly escalate the hot passion in both the man and the woman.

To fully experience this maximum skin contact, drizzle a little warming massage oil between your bodies and experience one of the best co-created massages ever. Have a big towel under him, though, because this position can get hot and messy!

In the Reverse Pressing Position, the woman can control a lot of the action. She can rub her body on his, clinch and release his penis between her legs and thighs, caress, kiss, and control the rhythm and timing of their orgasms. Her breasts get a lot of stimulation, and he'll love the feel of her erect nipples brushing back and forth on his chest.

> *"My husband is such a mountain of a man that when I'm on top in the Reverse Pressing Position, we're able to make love for long periods of time without either of us getting tired. Once we establish a rocking rhythm, we can go forever!"*
>
> *—Lisa, 34*

Rule of Love

In the Pressing Positions the clitoris is much more likely to get stimulated as the lovers move up and down on each other's bodies and establish a rhythm that will take them both to ecstasy.

REAR PRESSING POSITION

The Rear Pressing Position is a vulnerable position for a woman, as she has to trust and surrender control of the movement and depth of penetration to the man. She has to like being "taken" from the rear. This is not recommended when the man's body is very large.

To begin this position, the woman lies on her stomach with her legs out straight and rather close together. He slowly puts his weight on her as she allows his penis to enter her. The woman can grab his penis with her buttocks and PC muscles and squeeze rhythmically. He can slowly thrust, grind his hips in circles, and rub up and down on her buttocks.

This is another good position for a man who has a rather large penis. He'll get great friction up and down his shaft when she squeezes her buttocks together on each of his outstrokes during thrusting. The woman can stimulate her clitoris by slipping her hand under her hips and sliding two of her fingers over her clitoris so that it is between her fingers. As the man thrusts, the movement will transfer to her body and she'll slip back and forth on her wet fingers and build her passion to the boiling point.

THE CRAB POSITION

The Crab Position is very nurturing, but its erotic nature is very strong, too! The woman's arms and legs are wrapped around the man's body, holding him close. He is encircled and grasped by her love and her passion, lying in her arms in the Crab Position.

Both lie on their sides, facing each other. The man enters the woman as she opens her legs and simultaneously wraps her legs around his hips and thighs to bring him closer. Her foot gives her traction so that she can move to her own satisfaction.

The woman can initiate thrusting with her top leg by pulling him closer and releasing him with her foot. As she rocks her pelvis, a passionate rhythm can evolve. He can thrust as she rocks by pulling and releasing his pelvis. A couple that really explores this position will figure out how to have the man alternate between deep thrusts and shallower, more G-spot-friendly thrusts. She can control the energy, depth, and rhythm of the thrusting. Both can use their hands freely to scratch, caress, and tease different erogenous zones while playing in the passionate embrace.

VARIATION ON THE CRAB POSITION

Begin the Variation on the Crab Position by getting into the Crab Position. Lie down facing each other, with him between her legs so she can "pinch" him like a crab! Once both are comfortable, the woman raises her top leg. This allows him deeper access to her.

She can hold her upper leg with her hand and maneuver it to her liking. This movement also adjusts the angle of penetration to give her G-spot more pleasure.

If he is the one to hold her leg up, the dance is even hotter. When the man supports her leg, he can use it for resistance so that he can really get some swing to his hips. If he grasps her leg just above the knee he can lift her hips slightly as he thrusts, again sensually pleasuring her G-spot and vagina with his in-and-out motions, as well as the side-to-side ones.

> *"It's so hot when my partner takes control! I love feeling 'taken' by him. It's perfect when I'm in my head thinking about something else and he just takes over. I love surrendering to the feeling."*
> *—Angelina, 28*

STANDING POSITIONS

Positions of the standing variety are found in abundance carved in stone on certain temples in India. The most famous temples that are still standing are in the cities of Khajaraho, Orissa, and Konorak. The beautifully carved structures are all at least a thousand years old. The imagination runs wild to fantasize the rituals and sexual ceremonies that took place in these holy temples so very long ago.

Standing positions are described in the *Kama Sutra* as being *chitra*, or "amusing." This is because they are usually chosen when the couple is in a jovial mood. They are fun positions to try, but caution needs to be taken to not hurt oneself in the name of sex. Unless both partners are in top shape, the best way to start with standing positions is to try them in water. The mid-body depth of a warm pool would be perfect.

BAMBOO STALKS ENTWINED

Both the man and the woman stand equal, facing each other, and begin this position by kissing and eye gazing. Once harmonized energetically, the woman steps to one side of her lover and their legs alternate. She lifts one of her legs so that he can enter her with his erect penis. She then sets her leg down and they subtly adjust for comfort.

This position has the rare ability to actually rub the woman's clitoris. The upper part of his shaft touches her clitoris, so even gentle thrusting will stimulate it. If his penis is of the type that stands and points upward, this position should work very well. Being of equal height is very good, but if he is much taller than she is, Bamboo Stalks Entwined is not a good position to try.

The couple's hands can massage each other's buttocks, waist, and side areas under the arms while they hold each other close. Leverage can be gained by pressing their bodies together using their hands. This is a sweet position that requires little effort. It may be best to try this one first as a preliminary to other, more vigorous standing positions.

SUSPENDED POSITION

To begin the Suspended Position, the man should lean against a wall or against one of the sides in a doorway. He'll have much better balance and control if he positions his feet well away from the wall, so that his legs are angled from his hips and not straight. This adjustment creates a bit of a lap in which his partner can sit. This position requires a strong man, since he will be fully supporting his partner's weight.

The woman stands before him and puts her arms around his shoulders and neck. He lifts one of her legs by sliding it over his forearm and onto his elbow. As she helps by lifting herself with her arms, he lifts the other leg up and into the crook of his other arm. After a few wiggles for adjustment, he can pull her closer and begin to thrust. If they are both strong enough, she can put her feet on the wall behind him and push to help with the thrusting.

If movement is difficult, the couple can do this position in relative stillness, without a lot wild thrusting. A woman who has strong PC muscles can contract and release them to create pleasure for both. This is also true for the man. Both can squeeze and release their PC muscles in rhythm while he gently pulls her to him in small, thrusting sequences.

THE THREE STEPS OF VISHNU

The Three Steps of Vishnu is a position from the *Ananga Ranga*. It is a fairly easy position and actually has some interesting possibilities for erotic pleasure.

The couple should stand on a firm surface, face to face, with their legs alternating. The woman then raises one leg and he holds on to it, around the thigh or calf area, and pulls her close. She embraces him so that they are as close as possible.

With her leg up they can achieve a greater depth of penetration. The man can use his grip on her leg to move her body back and forth on him. This can be a sideways motion or, more traditionally, a forward and backward motion. The grip on her leg allows for the two to move in unison. The woman should choose which leg she wants to have held up, depending on her knowledge of her G-spot and her preferences for depth and motion.

Variations include the woman putting her raised leg up on a thick cushion or stool. If the woman is much shorter than the man, she can stand on a small stool or on a step to raise her up.

> "My wife and I love to have standing sex in the shower after the kids are asleep, then we dry each other off and make love again in bed. We've used this position in my mother's bathroom once, and it worked! I think the fact that we felt pretty naughty both during and afterward helped add to the excitement."
>
> —Chris, 38

KNEE AND ELBOW POSITION

The Knee and Elbow Position, from the *Ananga Ranga*, would be great to first try in the water, especially if you haven't had practice with standing positions before. For the couple that can accomplish this position, it is quite a bit of fun. The woman has a lot of control, as long as the man has a good hold of her and doesn't lose his balance.

He stands and lifts her on to him with her legs over his inner elbows for support. She holds on around his neck and he clasps his hands together behind her waist to hold her firmly. They can swing and sway and get quite wild in this position if he is strong and she is light. It is natural for him to pull her close and then release her to facilitate deep thrusting. She can also pull herself up and down on his erect penis by squeezing and loosening her arms around his neck, thus creating different thrusting patterns and movements.

The Knee and Elbow Position is a good position for kissing, neck biting, and eye gazing because the two of you are very close. Their breasts rub together with each thrust, and the woman's clitoris may also experience some friction from the up-and-down movements and the fact that her legs are spread very wide.

PRESSED POSITION (PAGE 121)

HAND ON HEART POSITION
(PAGE 147)

VARIATION ON THE
CRAB POSITION (PAGE 103)

VARIATION ON
YAWNING POSITION (PAGE 66)

YAB YUM OR LOTUS POSITION
(PAGE 114)

MONKEY POSITION (PAGE 132)

ADVANCED
KAMA SUTRA POSITIONS

These more advanced *Kama Sutra* positions are for those times when you are feeling frisky and wild and are willing to stretch a little!

PACKED POSITION (PAGE 63)

ONE LEG UP POSITION (PAGE 67)

ALTERNATING FEET (PAGE 88)

SOARING AND FLUTTERING
BUTTERFLY (PAGE 89)

YONI YANTRA (PAGE 119)

> "We like to watch ourselves in the big mirror by our bed when we're making love. It's erotic and edgy to see yourself having lots of pleasure. At first I couldn't look but now I can't get enough of us!"
>
> −Anna, 29

GLORIOUS POSITION

What a name—the Glorious Position! It makes one want to try it just because of the name. This position is best assumed by a younger couple who are very fit and in the heights of passion.

The Glorious Position, from the *Ananga Ranga*, is similar to the Knee and Elbow Position above. The difference is that the man's legs are spread out very far for stability and his hands aren't locked behind the woman's back. One or both hands are placed under her buttocks and the other hand can be used to move her leg for added friction and movement. The woman holds on and helps swing and sway to his thrusting.

This position requires strength, even though the wide stance that the man adopts can help offset weight in this position. This one could also be done in a shallow pool, as the water will partially support the woman. With one hand on her sacrum he can push and hold her against his thrusting. Her legs are so wide apart that this is again a good position for deep penetration. It will also affect her G-spot favorably.

HAWKS MATING IN FLIGHT

Of all the standing positions illustrated thus far, Hawks Mating in Flight is the easiest and probably the most pleasurable position for the woman. It's all about stimulating the G-spot.

When looking at the photograph, imagine a cross-section of their bodies showing the top of his shaft pressing against her upper vaginal area near or right on the G-spot. The slight up-and-down motion of him lifting her buttocks will exact pleasure even with the absence of any thrusting.

Accessorize, accessorize, accessorize. Place pillows under her head, shoulders, upper back, and even her buttocks to make this position more comfortable. She can help hold herself up by hooking her feet on his shoulders and pressing her body to his.

To get into this position easily, start with her reclining on the bed. If the bed is too high for your bodies to meet comfortably, then try a couch or an overstuffed chair. While she relaxes on her back, he pulls her body toward him (closer to the edge of the bed). She then straightens her legs and he lifts her buttocks up toward his erect penis.

As he slides his erect penis into her, they can make small adjustments as needed. With his help, she slowly raises her legs up one at a time and rests them on his shoulders. This is a great position in which to gaze at one another and strike her G-spot.

The two move together to undulate and thrust. The woman has remarkable movement capabilities. In particular, she can rotate her hips in clockwise or counterclockwise movements, to both his and her delight. Because she is supporting herself on his shoulders, Hawks Mating in Flight isn't a very tiring position for either of you. You unite and mate in flight.

THE WHEELBARROW POSITION

This position is a modern one. Although there are no references to it in any of the ancient texts, it's such an exotic position that it just had to be included here. The Wheelbarrow Position is a difficult position, even for very fit couples with a great sense of humor!

Prepare some pillows and maybe a mat for the woman's shoulders, head, and hands so that she won't slip but has some comfortable items with which to pad herself. She kneels on the floor and her partner stands behind her. She lifts up, supporting herself with her hands, and the man carefully lifts one of her legs off the floor, and then the other so that he is eventually holding both of her legs at the ankles or calves.

He enters her and slides his hands up to her thighs to get a better hold. The woman can often find a way to hook her legs either under or over his arms to help support herself as he thrusts from his standing position.

This position requires a strong man and a strong woman, as she must hold herself up with her arms. An easier variation on this position would be for the woman to hold herself up on her forearms, from the hands to the elbow, and for the man to be on his knees rather than fully standing up, which is also a much less extreme angle.

Rule of Love

Standing positions are often great for men when it comes to lasting longer. Because they involve standing versus lying down, they give a kind of control and power to the man. He must exert some energy to remain standing, and so standing positions can help inhibit ejaculation.

6

Sitting and Other Exotic Positions

"In the opinion of Vatsyayana, just as variety is necessary in love, it is equally true that love is to be mutually aroused through variety. Hence, those courtesans who are clever and who are acquainted with the varieties of love-sport are generally more in demand. Thus, husbands and wives should engage in a variety of lovemaking techniques."

—Part 2, Chapter 4, Verse 25, the *Kama Sutra*

The positions that involve sitting or more upright postures are somewhat esoteric. Many require limber bodies and supple limbs, but that doesn't mean they are difficult. Couples experienced in Tantra, as well as those renowned for their *Kama Sutra* skills, consider the sitting positions magical and transformative. These exotic positions have the ability to enhance the sexual and sensual energy movement throughout the body. Some were said to have secret powers that only the very most skilled lovers could tap.

SITTING POSITIONS

The sitting positions are "awake" positions. With the man's penis pointing upward, the energy rises vertically, which allows the couple's bodies to move and wave freely. The breath of the partners can move in synchronicity, or they can do alternate breathing for best pheromone transmission. The hands of each partner support the other's body, and the man can easily control his urge to ejaculate by slowing their movement, breathing in his partner's essence, and resuming his movements when he has gained control.

YAB YUM OR LOTUS POSITION

The Yab Yum Position is the classical Tantric position most revered by the lovers of the exotic arts. It is called the Lotus Position in the *Kama Sutra*. The many ancient statues, paintings, and drawings attest to the power of this position. The great Indian god and goddess couple, Shiva and Shakti, sit in this position as they reign over the universe and all within it. They are the supreme male and female energies, and this is their position.

The next time you are feeling like a god and goddess, try this position. Create a comfortable area on which to sit. It should be firm but soft, and several pillows should be available to put under both the man and the woman's buttocks. A pillow under her buttocks will give her a little more height to meet his penis and will take the pressure off of his legs a bit.

The man begins by sitting cross-legged and his lover sits astride him, facing his inviting chest. The woman wraps her legs around him and embraces him with her arms. She holds him such that one hand is around his neck and one is at his lower back, so that she can pull him closer. He mimics her hand placements, as he tenderly caresses her lower back, just above her buttocks slit. Their breasts, mouths, pelvises, and genitals are in perfect alignment.

The Yab Yum Position allows the couple to rock and roll! They each use their hands on the sacrum of the other to push gently as they rise and fall with the steady tide of powerful erotic energy. As the perspiration beads form on their glistening bodies, they fall further into a rhythm, tightening their grips and plunging eagerly over and over as they consume each other in passionate rapture.

Their hands are free to fondle, caress, hold, and stroke each other. The man's mouth has perfect access to her erect

nipples for sucking and licking. He can heighten her deep pleasure by nibbling and sucking them as he leans her back and then slides her forward, over his bursting penis. The hands help create a wave of thrusting that enhances the rocking motion of this position. It is easy to stay enraptured for hours in this thrilling position!

"My husband and I love the Yab Yum Position because we can go for so long together. In this deep embrace we kind of enter into a trance that makes us feel like we've melted together."

—Tara, 35

MODIFIED YAB YUM

This version, the Modified Yab Yum, is fantastic for couples that aren't quite as flexible as they once were. It is also great for men with lower back problems who find sitting in the yoga posture of Yab Yum more difficult. This modified version is versatile and can be done anywhere there is a suitable chair!

Begin by choosing a great location, around your home or maybe even outdoors. Get out of the bedroom and change your point of view. Invite your lover to sit in a plush chair or lounge as you climb onto his lap and into his lustful, waiting arms. Again, you can use a pillow to raise her buttocks up a bit and ease the pressure on his legs. Each of your hands goes to the other's lower back and neck so that you can hold and rock to your hearts' content.

If the chair has a back to it, the woman can push against the back of the chair with her feet, instead of wrapping them around her man. This will help with the thrusting and pelvic rocking that can be so passionate in this position. She can also hold on to the back of the chair for easy rocking. Each partner can kiss, nibble, and suck the other's neck. They can kiss with wet, juicy lips and caress and fondle almost any body part with their free hands. Her breasts are ready and waiting for his tender, writhing tongue.

The man can move his legs in and out to create another kind of wave of movement. The woman's buttocks will fall and then rise again as he opens and closes his legs, causing him to plunge deeper into her voluptuousness each time. Putting a little bit of sensuous massage oil on each of their thighs will cause this movement to be oh-so-lusciously erotic and slippery!

ALL-AROUND POSITION

Begin the All-Around Position by finding a firm yet soft place to make love. The sand of a beautiful tropical beach would be a perfect place, but the bedroom can be great, too, as long as it has a romantic ambience about it. Have some pillows nearby for support and comfort. The man sits down and either sits up on his own or reclines gently against a wall, some pillows, or the bed frame. He should remain mostly upright if he is leaning against a support of some kind.

His woman straddles his lap, facing him, as he scoops up her legs at the thighs and lifts her onto his erect, waiting penis. The man slides her closer, with his hands on her thighs, as she throws her arms around his shoulders and hangs on. For the woman who is voluptuous, place firm pillows under her buttocks to lift her slightly. If the woman is of a smaller size, the man can tighten his grip around her legs, with his elbows under her knees, clasp his hands together behind her back, and lift her easily up and down upon his erect penis.

While the woman may need her arms to hold on in this very passionate position, she can free them periodically to run her fingers through his hair, pull and fondle his earlobes, kiss his neck and lips, and scratch his shoulders and back. Scratching, as you'll learn in chapter 8, is an erotic way to up the sexual ante. It is used either in the height of passion or to increase passion at any given moment.

THE LOUNGE

Begin this position, the Lounge, by finding a perfect chair or couch upon which to "lounge." Make sure it is against a wall or firm on the ground so it doesn't slip out from under the woman during vigorous thrusting! This is a good position for giving the woman an orgasm or two with oral sex before entering her.

Have your lover sit on the edge of the chair and relax as you kneel in front of her gorgeous body. You massage the inside of her thighs as you spread her moist lips and enter her. Holding on to her thighs, the man uses his hands to support her while he thrusts into her writhing body, enjoying the ride as they go. An alternative position is to have the woman wrap her legs around her lover's hips as they thrust.

The man's hands are free to caress and massage her body, and he can fondle her clitoris, neck, earlobes, breasts, and nipples easily in this position. She can massage her own breasts and rub his chest, and teasingly pull his hair and scratch his arms as they wildly press their bodies together again and again.

EXOTIC AND ADVANCED POSITIONS

What position isn't exotic to someone who has never tried it? As you move through this book and the amazing selection of positions, note which aspects you like about certain positions and which aspects you love. Some positions won't work for certain couples, and others will be pleasurable beyond belief. So take note and try as many as you can to truly find the passionate delight that is possible for you. Life is short—use it to its fullest advantage. Try everything!

The positions that follow are some of the author's favorites. They have an otherworldly aspect that can carry you away to realms you didn't know existed. They have the potential to transform what you thought lovemaking was all about.

YONI YANTRA

The most ancient art symbol of the vagina is the triangle or V. This position personifies this concept. The Yoni Yantra Position is an ecstatic G-spot position. It allows the woman to be the mistress of her own pleasure when it comes to vaginal orgasms and deep, passionate lovemaking.

At the height of passion, when both the man and the woman are fully aroused, and the action turns to the more wild side, lie your lustful woman down on her back and make her comfortable. She then raises her legs and holds them in the air as the man approaches her voluptuous body. The woman spreads her legs apart while keeping them very high with her feet far forward toward her head.

The man kneels with his knees spread wide at her temple, bends slightly over her, and inserts his waiting penis. The woman adjusts her body to his and, in doing so, rises up even higher as his body puts pressure on her legs. She uses this pressure to hold herself up. She can push against his chest to help with the thrusting, timing, and depth of penetration. By pushing with her hands the woman can further position her body for the best G-spot angle. Her legs can be further forward, away from his chest, as she grinds and thrusts against the man's thrusting.

Fondling and caressing, the woman can stimulate her lover's arms, chest, neck, and face. She can teasingly pull the hair on his chest, adding excitement and pleasure to his experience. The man can sit back on his feet and change the angle of penetration, thereby letting her relax a little before they again plunge full force into their passionate embrace. Eye gazing, breathing together, and whispering hot, erotic suggestions to each other comes naturally in this position!

SPLITTING A BAMBOO

This classic position is extraordinary for both lovers. It is a supreme position for G-spot stimulation and is one in which the man can pace himself in order to have multiple waves of pleasure. It is rhythmic, erotic, and very physical.

After a long session of foreplay in which he lavishes her vulva and clitoris with many wet kisses and flicks of his tongue, the man should lie his lover down on her back. As he approaches her, the woman places one of her legs on his shoulder and the other one out to the side of her body. He straddles her lifted leg with his thighs and gently enters her.

The woman can dangle her leg that is to the outside in the air or she can rest it on pillows or the bed, as she pleases. Where she places that leg affects how her G-spot will be stimulated. She can play with this angle, and as things really heat up she can gently bounce it out to her side to get the action going during thrusting. This can be a wild ride! This position calls for changing the leg that is up on his shoulder frequently so that all the areas of her vagina get stimulated.

All hands are free in this position except for maybe the hand he uses to hold her leg close to his body. Either lover can fondle and manipulate her clitoris from this position. They can caress, scratch, nibble, and suck each other's toes, legs, stomachs, breasts, and pubic mounds. An extra erotic treat is that the man can watch the rhythmic quivering of her breasts as he plunges again and again into his beloved.

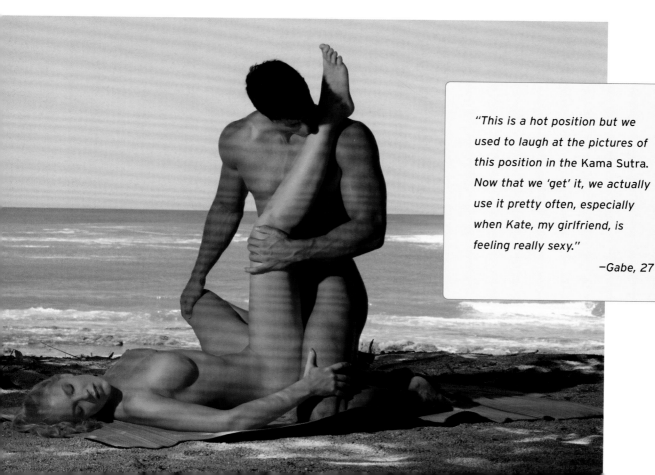

"This is a hot position but we used to laugh at the pictures of this position in the Kama Sutra. Now that we 'get' it, we actually use it pretty often, especially when Kate, my girlfriend, is feeling really sexy."

—Gabe, 27

Churning, which was briefly discussed in chapter 3, "Man Superior Positions," is another thrusting technique described in the *Kama Sutra*. It can be done in one of two ways. The man's hips can grind in circles while he is inside his lover, or he can use his hand on his penis to "churn" his shaft inside of his lover. This movement is stimulating to both partners.

Thrusting techniques will help the man last longer while focusing your attention on her pleasure. You'll begin to be able to read her reactions and arousal better and tune your lovemaking to bring her to ecstasy every time. Keeping track of your thrusts will help you from going over the top too soon.

PC MUSCLES FOR FABULOUS LOVEMAKING

While exercising your PC (puboccygeous) muscles is an age-old sex secret that was documented in the *Kama Sutra*, it wasn't until the 1950s that the practice became better known when the American gynecologist, Arnold Kegel, realized the benefit of exercising this love muscle—thus the reason why these exercises are now called Kegels.

Strengthening your PC muscles so that you can perform the Pair of Tongs can yield numerous benefits for lovemaking. Strong pelvic floor muscles will build your orgasmic potential, tighten your bladder, and increase the strength of your orgasms. You will find that using your strong muscles during sex will increase your pleasure for you and your lover. Some of you may want to amaze your partner with ancient feats from the sixty-four arts of the *Kama Sutra*. Strong PC muscles are also indicated in female ejaculation and ejaculation mastery for men.

A healthy, fit, and limber body responds best to the demands the owner may put on it during great sex. Whether it's vigorous or meditative sex, strong pelvic muscles are essential. Orgasms become stronger when the PC muscles are healthy and strong.

Women often mention that the girth of the penis is more important to them than the length. Again, this is hardly important if the woman is practicing her PC muscle, or Kegel, exercises. She is relying on the man to fill up a vagina that may have gotten weaker over the years and is, therefore, not as tight a fit as it once might have been. It is to the woman's benefit that she develops stronger PC muscles. Not only will she be more satisfied with any size penis, but she will also have much more sexual vitality and orgasmic potential.

THE BASIC PC, OR KEGEL, EXERCISE

You'll be isolating your pelvic floor muscles for these exercises. They can be done almost anywhere, and at any time, once you've mastered them. Though it may sound daunting now, you'll want to work up to about 200 a day. This will take about five or six minutes once a day. You can do them at your desk for a little pick-me-up during your workday or while driving your car or sitting on the bus. The time is well worth it, and you'll always notice afterward that you feel turned on!

The first thing you'll want to do is find out where exactly these muscles are. Go into your bathroom and sit on the toilet. Start to urinate and stop the flow before you are done. Try it again. Those are the muscles with which you'll be working. Once you can isolate them you'll be ready to start the practice.

Begin by squeezing like you did while finding your muscles on the toilet. Try to leave your anal muscles out of the practice for now. To begin with you may not be able to isolate these from the rest of your pelvic floor muscles. You'll be able to do that soon enough, so, for now, know that eventually you'll want to focus on just the front muscles that stop the flow of urine.

It is important to relax fully between each squeeze. Squeeze . . . relax . . . squeeze . . . relax . . . and so on. Start slowly. You'll be building up your speed eventually, once you can do these naturally. Only do about twenty-five the first time you try these. You may hurt the next day. It will go away soon, so keep it up. Add more each week until you can quickly sustain around 200 squeezes. Remember to breathe deeply while you're doing the exercises.

PC MUSCLE EXERCISES FOR MEN

Men have some options for doing their PC muscle exercises. At first you should start by having a flaccid penis. Just tighten and relax as the above instruction indicates. Eventually you can do these when you are aroused and erect. They get really fun then because you can see a bit more of the action! Your penis will be bouncing and banging up and down wildly.

When you do the advanced sets of sustained, slow Kegels, you'll be able to watch your penis as it rises upward and then, as you let go, falls into a more relaxed state. An even more advanced practice is to put weights on your penis. You can

The Art of Love

Pompoir is the art of the woman "milking" the penis of the man. There have been women throughout history who have been known for their amazing sexual prowess. Some have even had such strong vaginal muscles that they could hold on to a man's penis while he was inside of them and not let him out. Strong PC muscles are the key to pompoir.

do this simply by draping a dry washcloth over your hard shaft while you are sexercising. As you get good at this, you can wet the washcloth a bit to add more weight. This is going to make you an incredible lover!

PC MUSCLE EXERCISES FOR WOMEN

Women have some extra things they can do to help strengthen their pelvic floor muscles, too. Once you've started your sexercises, you'll begin to notice that you can isolate the groups of muscles that are holding up your pelvic floor. You'll be able to flick your clitoral, anal, or vaginal set of muscles simply by putting your mind to it. This is beneficial when you want to turn yourself on a little. Just move or rapidly pump the clitoral hood over your clitoris fifty times to stimulate yourself!

If you decide to really get into these sexercises, you can purchase a vaginal weight lifting egg or one of the many Kegel squeezing toys that are on the market. You can visit www.babeland.com and www.goodvibes.com for a variety of items for this purpose. Holding the somewhat heavy eggs in is a challenge, as are working with the devices made for measuring the strength of your muscles. Some of these are medically approved, but they may be more high tech than you need. They are somewhat stimulating to have inside of you, but don't forget to take them out when you've finished!

> "I'm a weight lifter, so I'm in pretty good shape, but when I started doing Kegel exercises it put a whole different perspective on weight lifting! I stay hard longer and I can make love for an amazing amount of time now."
>
> —Stephan, 36

7

Interpretations from Nature

"An ingenious person should multiply the kinds of congress after the fashion of the different kinds of beasts and of birds. For these different kinds of congress, performed according to the usage of each country, and the liking of each individual, generate love, friendship, and respect in the hearts of women."

—Part 2, Chapter 6, Verses 48-49, the *Kama Sutra*

OUR ANIMAL NATURE

The society that created the *Kama Sutra* believed that man was simply a part of the larger whole of creation. They knew that although man has some superior qualities, humans cannot be separated from everything else in the world—everything we see, hear, smell, touch, and feel. Our erotic nature can, in many ways, be likened to that of the birds and the beasts. Therefore, it was suggested that animals and their sexual nature be studied to inform lovers of interesting ways to make love.

There is a certain humor to the names that have been ascribed to some of the positions that follow. While most of us don't think of ourselves as animals, it is instructional to enjoy our more animal-like nature by attempting some of the postures and attitudes that animals display. Who's to say you can't roar like a lion when you feel empowered or particularly amorous? Why not playfully bite or suck your lover's neck during intercourse? Wrapping your legs and arms around your lover and squeezing tightly like an anaconda can be exciting and endearing. Nibbling at your lover's eyelids and cheeks like a bird could be a great way to tell him you're ready for love.

All too often we modern humans deny that we are a part of nature. This can put a hold on letting go in the bedroom. You have many erogenous zones all over your body that you may never think of taking advantage of during sex. The underarms, sides of the torso, toes, fingers, necks, and ears, and the places where we have hair on our bodies, are all filled with nerve endings that provide an opportunity to feel much more during lovemaking. If you pay greater attention to these areas, your erogenous zones will inform your loving and add a sense of discovery to it, too.

It might be fun to take a trip to the zoo or the county fair with your lover, or watch nature programs on television, to observe animals and see whether you can detect any clues to new positions and suggestive techniques you might try out later. Make love outside sometime when you are camping, or at the beach on a day when no one else is present. Make a love nest in your backyard if you have a private one. Risk trying something a little different. You'll benefit by adding excitement to your lovemaking, and you'll feel more connected with nature.

> *"I love having sex with my boyfriend when I'm sitting on his lap. I put my arms around his neck, lean back, and we immediately get into rhythm. I can really feel his strength, kiss his face, and dance deliriously in his lap. It's the one position I come in the most."*
>
> —Rainey, 2

FRONTAL POSITIONS INSPIRED BY NATURE

The selection of positions that follows is fancifully inspired by the natural habits of animals. These positions focus on couples facing each other during lovemaking. The wise lover remembers that animals tend to have elaborate mating rituals that precede the actual act of sex. Thrilling courtship displays might be likened to romantic notes, sensual massages by candlelight, or flowers and chocolates, for no particular occasion other than to love, honor, and court your partner. What exotic courting behaviors can you think of?

MONKEY POSITION

The Monkey is a position for the height of passion, when the sexual energy is running on the wild side. Women's breasts, particularly the nipples, are very sensitive to touch and will often flush a red color when sexual excitement is high. Gently slapping or caressing the area between the breasts can be stimulating, as it is the Heart center and the home of the thymus gland, which plays an important part in a healthy immune system.

Approach this position by having the man fold his knees and sit on his thighs. He should help his partner onto his lap by placing his arms under her legs to guide her up onto his erect penis (this requires some strength on the part of the man). She can begin by putting her arms around his neck until they get a good rhythm going.

The man uses his arms and his pelvis to create a forward and backward motion. An in-and-out, rather than a side-to-side, motion is called for in this position. As they find their rhythm, she can release one of her arms from around his neck and caress his chest with either the back of her hand or her flat palm, as desired. She can caress her own breasts or go back and forth between the two of them. This action can serve as a metaphor for the Heart connection between two lovers—a reminder to Love and to be in the Heart.

The man can also initiate the caressing. He readjusts the position and releases one of her legs. However, in doing so, the angle of penetration will slightly tilt to one side or the other. This can be very positive for his partner, as many women know that their G-spots are just ever so slightly to one side or the other. By knowing this intimate detail, a man can adjust the angle of his penetration and release one of his hands to gently slap her chest or thigh or to touch his lover in whatever way might be arousing to her.

Upright positions like this one are good for the G-spot. The penis is upright and pressed against the woman's pubic bone from inside. The back-and-forth motion will cause the head of the penis to come in contact with her G-spot on the outstroke, before he thrusts deeper into her on the instroke.

The Monkey is also a good position for ejaculation mastery because the man is in almost complete control of the movement. If he finds himself getting too turned on and about to climax, he can come to stillness easily in this position. The couple breathes together and remains still so the man can resume a more active role within minutes. She can gently stimulate him by using her strong PC muscles to squeeze and release his penis, thereby keeping him alert and ready for more.

TORTOISE POSITION

In the Tortoise Position the couple sits upright, which gives an energizing flow to their lovemaking. To begin, the man sits comfortably on the bed or on a soft pad on the floor. His partner straddles his lap and sits on top of him, facing his chest. It may help to have a firm pillow under her buttocks for this position to ease the pressure on the man's legs.

The woman puts her feet on the bed or floor next to the man's thighs, just beyond his knees. She holds him close and he wraps his arms around her. Their breasts, genitals, mouths, hearts, eyes, and lips all meet in alignment. She uses her thighs and feet to rise up and down on his very erect penis. She can flick her hips back and forth over him or they can rock together to create a motion that locks them in a passionate embrace and increasingly vigorous experience. They can then slow their passion and rock gently or vibrate in stillness for a few minutes while they regain their composure, only to take up the act again.

Writers of the *Kama Sutra* era said that this posture helps circulate energy and holds the secret to longevity for both lovers. Is that living a long time or lasting a long time? Hours of hot, erotic sex are just what the doctor ordered!

Strong PC muscles are of benefit to both the man and the woman in this position. As they rest, they can both squeeze and release their genitals to keep them both aroused. The arms and hands of both partners are free to fondle, massage, and stroke each other.

Rule of Love

A particular kind of thrill is to softly, erotically, touch your lover's face, eyes, lips, cheeks, ears, and neck with tender fingertips. Touch so lightly and lovingly that you can barely feel your fingertips. These are the special things everyone needs and cares about: to be nurtured erotically!

BIRD POSITION

Many birds mate from a frontal position and often in the air. You'll most likely stay grounded on the bed for this one, though orgasmically you are bound to soar!

Begin the Bird Position by having the woman lie back on the bed comfortably with a few pillows behind her to slightly recline her body so she can see her partner while they make love. The man sits between her legs and bends his knees so that his feet have some traction. She raises her legs and places them under his arms so that they are on either side of his waist. He plunges into her as he pulls her toward him for closer contact. His arms can be at her waist or her hips for pulling her lower body close.

Thrusting from this position requires that the man be somewhat agile as he rocks on his feet and buttocks to initiate sexual congress. The woman can move her hips by gently thrusting to his rhythm or she can grind her hips in circles like a churning river at flood stage. Squeezing her knees around his waist pulls him closer for deeper penetration as he caresses her breasts, nipples, and clitoris with his free hands. If they wrap their arms around each other's necks, they will be approaching the next position, the Advanced Bird Position.

"When she is on my lap, we are breathing the same air and this delicious vapor rises from where we are joined. I also like the sound of our thighs slapping together and her breath in my ear. My lover is so beautiful when she is in bliss."

—Ken, 38

ADVANCED BIRD POSITION

The Advanced Bird Position begins by warming up and increasing arousal in the Bird Position discussed above. The natural inclination will arise to move closer together for a deeper embrace. The man can rise up on his a feet as he moves to the more intimate posture. This will give him more leverage for thrusting and allow him deeper access to her vagina.

As the couple moves closer, her legs move from below his arms to above them. He now wraps his arms behind her knees and reaches his hands for her upper body. As he presses his body closer to hers, he pushes her legs to her chest. (Her legs must be very flexible to do this kind of bending.) The closer they are, the more open and inviting her vagina is. A sensuous nibble on the neck or ear can add another element of pleasure.

The man can thrust deeply into the woman as he embraces and kisses her. His penis will certainly stimulate her G-spot, as she is wide open and accessible. An experienced and loving partner knows that if he employs a variety of thrusting techniques he will see her eyes open wide and her skin flush crimson with pleasure. Shallow thrusting combined with a well-placed deeper thrust now and then should do the trick!

CRANES WITH NECKS INTERTWINED

This beautiful and loving posture, Cranes with Necks Intertwined, is less active than many others. It is a good position for a man who has a large penis, because his lover can manage the depth of thrusting from on top as she uses her knees to rise up and down on his shaft.

To engage in this position, the man should sit on the bed with his legs bent underneath him and slightly apart at the feet. He may wish to put a firm, small pillow under his buttocks to support his legs. His lover climbs onto his lap, facing him, and can have her legs either out in front of her or her knees on the bed for better traction.

The woman's arms encircle his neck and they bring their heads, necks, and chests close to each other, as if dancing cheek to cheek. The man grasps her sweet buttocks with his hands to assist her in rising up and down on his erect penis. If the woman is on her feet or her knees she can help with the up-and-down motions. He can caress her buttocks, torso, and breasts while thrusting and plunging in and out of her.

Try swinging to and fro in this position. The man can lean forward a bit and then back, as if swinging. That motion will cause his shaft to pull in and

out and sweep past her G-spot. She can squeeze her PC muscles as he pulls out each time and relax them on his deep strike inward.

Upright positions like this one are good for restful pleasure. After some vigorous lovemaking, the couple can slow down and softly rock and squeeze together to keep the energy going. Breathing together, relaxing, kissing, and caressing can be enjoyed to keep the passion up but quiet down the urge to ejaculate.

REAR-ENTRY POSITIONS INSPIRED BY NATURE

These next selections are really nature-inspired sex. The erotic explorers of the past knew well that nature has things it can teach us—and what things those are! *National Geographic* is a great source for erotic positions from nature. You can often find programs that portray mating and sexual display.

Rear-entry positions are big favorites with many men and women alike because there are so many features that titillate the man and make the passion rise in the woman. If you haven't ventured to try rear-entry positions, now is the time to experience their erotic nature— and yours!

DEER POSITION

The Deer Position is voluptuous, sensual, and thrilling. It is one of the best positions for G-spot stimulation. The nature of the sentiment it produces is lustful and exciting to all involved. It's a great position on the bed, but do try it in other locations, too. A lush outdoor location, softened by the glow of the afternoon light, would make an experience that includes this position sizzling hot.

To begin, the woman puts her hands on the mat or bed in front of her so that she is on "all fours"—her weight supported by her hands and knees. She raises her buttocks invitingly as her lover, who is on his knees behind her, enters her from the rear. His hands are free to caress her buttocks and to massage her inner thighs and lower back.

The man stays upright in this position, though he may bend over his beloved, reaching to fondle her breasts and nipples or stroke her sides down to her waist. She can arch and undulate her

> ### Rule of Love
>
> In any of the rear-entry positions it may be an erotic turn-on to see yourselves in a mirror. Keep one near your bed for that purpose. When the time is right, bring it out and look at yourselves in the mirror. To see yourself and your lover's face in such pleasure is an edgy experience and powerful, too.

back to transfer movement to their genitals or bump and grind in rhythm to his thrusting. His hands can pull her closer for deeper penetration, and she can reach his scrotum and fondle and tease his balls with one of her hands quite easily, too.

For an even more lustful experience, the woman can reach up and hold onto the wall or bedstead in front of her. This changes the angle of penetration and for some women sends them over the top to orgasm. The G-spot is affected in any of the rear-entry positions, but this one puts a bit more of an angle on the penis-vagina fit that enlivens the flow of energy.

LION POSITION

The Lion Position is a sensual, languid human version of the real thing. This is a relatively relaxing position because the woman is on her stomach and chest with her body turned slightly to admire and embrace her lover.

Start by having the woman lie flat on her stomach on the bed. She brings one leg up in a stepping motion to her side as she turns slightly to eye gaze with her partner. The man kneels behind her and seductively teases her with his erect penis. As he enters her he moves forward so that his arms and face come closer to hers.

The woman's arm can reach for the man's shoulder as she's twisting, and

hold on to him, as they look into each other's eyes. The twist in her body, and the rising of her hips to meet his, allows for deep penetration and mutual stimulation.

A male lion will grab his mate's neck and hold on, as if biting her. This is to hold her steady, but you can do it to stimulate and excite your lover. Nibble at her neck, bite her ear, and suck her fingers as you mount her, striking deeply each time you thrust, bite, thrust, and suck. She, in turn, can fondle your scrotum and drive her pelvis, undulating and writhing in pleasure.

POSITION OF A COW

The Cow Position is a standing position. It is one of the most well known of the *Kama Sutra* animal positions, and it is named after the animal that is the darling of Indian culture—the cow. These animals are holy in the Hindu religion; none can be killed and all are to be revered. It is a sacred position.

Begin by having the woman stand and bend over so that her hands are supporting her on the floor in front of her or on a low table or chair. Her man steps in from behind her and, as she presents herself to him, he mounts her and clasps his hands around her waist to bring her body and buttocks close to him so that he can thrust lustfully.

Men like to see their lover's backside. The round, firm buttocks remind him of her breasts and, because he can see everything that is going on, he is in heaven. Thrusting patterns are easy in this position and should be employed liberally. Rubbing massage oil on her back and buttocks is a fantastic way to build the eroticism of the moment.

The woman can easily reach between his legs to caress his scrotum and balls, and he can fondle her breasts when he is in a cooling-down period and not thrusting so vigorously. The man can rise up on his toes and then drop back down in a rhythmic motion, or she can do the same. Another variation of this position has the woman lift one of her legs up to the man's waiting hand. He holds it alongside his waist or under his arm as they continue to enjoy each other. The choice of legs depends on the woman's knowledge of her G-spot and what she likes.

VARIATION ON THE POSITION OF THE COW

This position, the Variation on the Position of the Cow, starts in the Position of the Cow. As the woman and man enjoy each other, she shifts her feet so that one of them moves forward, ahead of the other foot. This allows for deep penetration and enables her to look around to see her shining lover.

The location of her G-spot will determine which foot she moves forward to change the stimulation in her vagina as she pleases. If a few pillows or a low table or stool are used for her to rest her hands upon, she won't get tired from bending over. This position may also be done with

her leaning over the edge of the bed.

These last two positions invite the opportunity for anal play. Should your lover like that kind of stimulation, have a good-quality lubricant at hand so that your actions are seamless and you won't have to leave her for a moment. Massage and nibble her lower back, hips, and buttocks first, and then proceed to fondle her anus and surrounding tissue with your hands and fingers. Many women love this kind of play and often it will send them over the top to orgasm with just some simple teasing. You may even want to use this posture for anal sex, but ask first!

ELEPHANT POSITION

The Elephant Position is the classic rear-entry position. It's erotically stimulating and very visual for the man. If you both want to see each other, the woman can hold a hand mirror in which to see her lover's face. Rear-entry positions are usually not the first position a couple gets into when they start to make love, but later on, when both partners are highly aroused, rear entry is a luscious choice.

Start this position by having the woman lie on her stomach on the bed. She should rise up on her knees while keeping her head, arms, and breasts on the bed. She displays her beautiful buttocks for her partner as he kneels behind her and enters her. As he rubs her buttocks and thighs and caresses her inner cheeks he can thrust vigorously or pace himself for a more controlled experience. As the turn-on increases, the woman may raise her buttocks even higher—a sign that she wants more aggressive action. This excites him, and he will lustfully accommodate her wishes!

If the woman has her knees inside of his, she can use her thigh muscles to squeeze his penis and also control the depth of penetration. She may move one leg or both to the outside, as this will expose her vagina for deeper penetration. She can also shift the position by lifting one leg so that he can hold it under his arm and maneuver his beloved with it, as well as reach her clitoris for fondling with his finger or penis. This movement also gives more direct pleasure in her G-spot area.

Reaching under the man with one hand and playing with his scrotum is easy for the woman from this position. If he sits down on his heels she can also reach his anus to pleasure him even more. Sometimes a man likes his prostate gland to be massaged and played with during sexual intimacy, and this is a great position for that. Pressing firmly on his perineum, the area between the base of his penis and his anus, is very pleasurable and will aid in keeping him from ejaculating too swiftly.

VARIATION ON THE ELEPHANT POSITION

This Variation on the Elephant Position is a more relaxing version than the previously illustrated Elephant Position. This is a vulnerable position for the woman because she is prevented from moving much and the angle of penetration can cause her cervix to be bumped if the man's penis is large or long. It is a great position if the man has a smaller organ, because it will give him deeper access.

To begin, the woman lies on her chest with a large, firm pillow under her hips. Her head is relaxed and down on the bed. The pillow is placed so that her

buttocks rise into the air and her thighs part slightly, to open her up in presentation to her lover. Her lover kneels down behind her and enters her. He can pull out from time to time to rub her vulva with his hand or hard penis, or even lick her labia.

He can place his knees either between her knees or on the outside of them, depending on what they like. If his knees are to the outside, her thighs will be closer together and she can squeeze his shaft more. The woman can pleasure her clitoris or she can reach up and gently pull and caress his balls.

HAND ON HEART POSITION

This variation on Moon-Gazing Turtledoves is very intimate and erotic for the lovers. It begins the same way as Moon-Gazing Turtledoves, with the man folding his legs and sitting on his feet. The woman straddles his lap, with her back to his chest, and then he enters her.

With the man's arms around his woman, they lift up onto their knees, at about a 45-degree angle from the bed. Once they have achieved the position, he places one hand between her breasts and the other on her abdomen, to facilitate rocking and thrusting. The lovers can rock back and forth together or the woman can rise and fall repeatedly onto his waiting shaft. He can flick his hips with short, quick thrusts as she follows his lead.

An interesting addition to the bedroom would be a simple bar or rings about 2 feet wide that can be hung from the ceiling just about arm's length above the woman. She can grab the bar and pull herself up into this position. The bar facilitates their coordinated movements, allowing her to be much more vigorous in her lusty plunging!

8

Enhancements to Lovemaking

"Sexual intercourse can be compared to a quarrel, on account of the contrarieties of love and its tendency to dispute. The place of striking with passion is the body, and on the body the special places are: the shoulders, the head, the space between the breasts, the back, the torso and the sides."

–Part 2, Chapter 7, Verses 1,2, the *Kama Sutra*

Beyond the positions for lovemaking there are a myriad of actions that completely transform the art of love. Part of the sixty-four arts from the *Kama Sutra* are erotic additions that most definitely increase sexual arousal. These arts allow for an adventurous spirit to come forth and make the journey of sex and love an individual experience. It is the combination of all of these arts that lays the foundation for an exquisite lover to be born and for a love relationship to form that is mythic in proportion.

COMMUNICATING—WORDS AND SOUNDS

The *Kama Sutra* suggests that the amorous couple mimic the sounds that the specific animals make when they are engaged in sex. Squeals, moans, grunts, chirps, roars, deep sighs, and purrs make the experience much more lively and allow the couple to forget about being inhibited so that they can expand and merge more easily. Communicating with your lover about what you like, how you like it, and when you like it is highly important. Partners are not mind readers, and they don't want to be, so let them know, in loving ways, what turns you on.

Erotic words are powerful stimulation for couples. Use your words liberally. Men tend to like lusty, more sexually explicit language, while women like more intimate, sensually suggestive and love-based words. Start your love play early in the day by dropping hints, leaving notes, making fantasy suggestions, and being liberal with compliments. The more you do this, the more turned on you'll both be when you get to the bedroom.

> *"It drives me divinely crazy when Susan moans during sex. It is such a great form of communication. I get chills and this kind of energy running all through my body when I can make her feel so much pleasure she doesn't know how to handle it. She just opens her mouth and lets it out!"*
> —Chris, 40

RITUALIZED SOUNDS AND STRIKING

The *Kama Sutra* details a whole series of highly ritualized sounds and expressions that will not be covered extensively here, but a taste of what was typical is offered. These sounds are tied to the set of arts called the Art of Striking. A formal structure of life and lovemaking isn't very appealing to modern lovers, but some of the practices might be, particularly to couples into light S&M.

The nerve bundles that carry both our pleasure and our pain impulses are woven around each other as they travel up and down our spines, which is why most people can stand much more pain when they are in the heights of sexual pleasure. Have you ever been in a new position during hot sex, and then suffered a little afterward? Your pleasure was concealing the pain. This is the same reason that some people like to play with pain during sex. Light spanking with soft leather whips or a hand can actually add to the erotic sentiment of the act of love, and natural cries and sounds are made during this kind of play, too.

The sutras go into detail about other cries that mean "stop" or "praise," as well as words that convey a "desire for liberation" at that moment. Praise and liberation have more to do with a kind of consciousness. It is tied to aspects of Tantric practice and is related to the release from the cycle of death and rebirth. Remember that the *Kama Sutra* was one of many "sciences" that was intertwined in Indian culture, so some of the positions and practices work in tandem with their other cultural sciences.

THE IMPORTANCE OF MAKING NOISE

These expressions don't apply in today's world but what does apply, however, is the idea of making noise when in ecstasy. It is actually very important and may make the difference for some women in whether they orgasm or not. Making deep, resonant sounds from the lower torso can result in multiple orgasms in both men and women.

Opening up the mouth and making sounds that are in the lower vocal range is important because it tends to release built-up energy in the body. It also expands the orgasmic potential by spreading the passion and turn-on throughout the body. This should be done during both the building of sexual energy and in the throes of orgasm. This is especially true if the mouth is open quite wide and the expression or sound that is produced comes from the belly or abdomen. This action opens up the central channel in the body that allows the ecstatic sexual wave to fill the entire body, thus creating whole body orgasms.

You can practice at times when you are by yourself, either self-pleasuring or any other time. If you find yourself at the beach, or hiking, or some other place where you won't feel intimidated by opening up and releasing sound, go for it! This especially may be a key to female ejaculation. Learning to open the body cavity in this way will help women expend their capacity for orgasm and ejaculation.

"My boyfriend and I were watching a Tantra video once and the woman in it was having wave after wave of orgasms. She was making deep sounds while this was happening. The next time we made love I tried copying her sounds and almost immediately I started to orgasm. I just couldn't believe it! It worked!"

—Ashley, 31

THE ART OF SCRATCHING

You have probably scratched your lover in the heat of passion before. The top of his head, his back, and his shoulders and arms are easily accessible during sexual contact. The *Kama Sutra* is, again, highly ritualized in its descriptions about this subject. Some of these marks and ideas are rather intriguing and might actually be applicable for you.

DIFFERENT TYPES OF SCRATCHING

According to the *Kama Sutra*, there are eight different kinds of scratching, depending on the marks that are produced:

Sounding: No scratch or mark is left, but only the hair on the body becomes erect from the touch of the nails, and only the nails themselves make a sound.

Half-moon: A semicircular, curved mark made with the nails, which is impressed on the neck and the breasts.

Circle: Half-moons that are impressed opposite each other.

Line: A straight line traced with the nails on any part of the body, but it must be short.

Tiger's Nail or Claw: A line curving inward, traced near the breasts or on the face.

Peacock's Foot: A curved mark made on the breast using the five nails.

Jump of a Hare: Five nail marks made close to one another near the nipple.

Leaf of a Blue Lotus: A mark made on the breast or on the hips in the form of a leaf of the blue lotus.

Rule of Love

Everyone scratches his or her lover at some point, but it usually just happens without any plan or reasoning. The next time you can actually think about using scratching as an aphrodisiac, try doing a more ritualized form of it. Four long fingernail prints embedded in his arm will have him remembering that special evening with you for weeks to come.

The *Kama Sutra* goes on to remark that the nail marks should not be made on a married woman unless they are hidden and she wants a remembrance of her lover, if he is to be gone for a period of time. The *Kama Sutra* also speaks of the respect that these nail marks carry, even if they are visible to strangers. Go ahead, it is absolutely all right to leave these marks on men, too!

THE ART OF BITING

Biting, along with scratching and embracing, was highly ritualized in ancient India at the time of the *Kama Sutra*. As you will see, it was a delicate art form and an integral part of the sixty-four arts of love.

All the places that can be kissed are also the places that can be bitten, except the upper lip, the interior of the mouth, and the eyes. The eight different kinds of biting are as follows:

Hidden Bite: The lower lip—shown only by the excessive redness of the skin—is bitten.

Swollen Bite: The lower lip is bitten on both sides.

The Point: A small portion of the skin—such as the lower lip—is bitten with two teeth only.

The Line of Points: Small portions of the skin—such as the throat, the armpit, the thighs, the joints of the thighs, and the forehead—are bitten with all the teeth.

The Coral and the Jewel: The same spot is squeezed several times between the top teeth—the jewel—and the lower lip—the coral.

The Line of Jewels: Biting is done with all the teeth.

The Broken Cloud: A circle of irregular small tooth marks is impressed beneath the breasts.

The Biting of the Boar: A wide area of bites are made close to one another, beneath the breasts, consisting of many broad rows with red intervals.

BREATH AND ORGASM

If there is one thing any person could do to improve his or her capacity for orgasm, it is relearning how to breathe. Proper breathing was an integral part of the Indian philosophy of Ayurveda—the ancient Hindu art of medicine and of prolonging life—and directly connected to vitality, health, and great sex. Many people don't know the basics about healthy breathing, let alone breathing that facilitates orgasm. We're a culture of chest breathers. Chest breathing causes adrenaline secretions that can lead to panic and fear, the fight-or-flight response. That's not a good thing if you want to make love, not war.

You can't relax your genitals when you're holding your stomach in. The body becomes rigid instead of flowing and relaxed. In contrast, it's pretty difficult to tighten and hold your genitals when your lungs are full and your stomach is relaxed. A relaxed body leads to a more relaxed, orgasmic experience. The way you breathe can make a vast difference in the quality of your orgasms and your life.

BELLY BREATHING PRACTICE

This is a simple but profound practice. Allow about 15 minutes for this exercise. Wear loose clothing without a belt and allow at least an hour since your last meal. Lie comfortably on the floor, on your back, in a quiet place where you won't be disturbed. Rest a few minutes and then begin to notice your breath. How are you breathing? Are you breathing through your mouth? Does your chest or your belly rise?

After you've briefly observed yourself, put your hands lightly on your abdomen and begin to breathe into your hands. Take long, slow breaths through your nose and visibly, but gently, force your belly to rise and fall with the breath. You may really have to focus on this pattern. Don't breathe into your chest. This will be difficult for some people and easier for others.

Practice this slow, steady breathing, being sure to observe the gentle rising of your abdomen. Take really deep breaths. Make them slow and deliberate. Slow them as much as possible. Keep this up for 10 minutes. Stay relaxed. Don't be frustrated with yourself if this is hard. You're in the process of learning something new and valuable. If this is easy for you, just focus your awareness on your belly and breath as a meditation practice.

ORGASM AND BREATH FOR WOMEN

Women who don't orgasm easily often hold their breath as they get more turned on. As they approach a kind of transition stage on the way to peak arousal, say a seven or an eight on a scale of one to ten, they will often hold their breath, and then the action stops. The result is that the orgasmic energy must build up again. Yet the same thing may happen repeatedly. Without deep breathing it becomes difficult to smoothly transition to the next level of sensations. The important thing is to keep breathing!

As arousal increases in women, they sometimes begin to breathe a little faster. This may start to occur at the level of a four or five on the scale of one to ten. If you can become aware of your breath, you can then begin to drive the experience by purposely practicing faster, focused breathing. This will increase the blood flow to your genitals and increase your arousal level, too. It helps, exactly as meditation does, to focus your energy with your breath and move from a sense of separateness to one of being merged with the sensual, erotic energy.

ORGASM AND BREATH FOR MEN

Men have different issues when it comes to breathing. They don't tend to hold their breath when they are excited, but they clamp down and stop breathing right before they are going to ejaculate. This is the time when they should keep breathing, but the breath needs to slow way down and become deeper and more relaxed. This helps prevent premature ejaculation and is the key to moving into the multiorgasmic state that men can achieve.

If you notice that you're holding your breath, breathing very fast, or tightening during lovemaking and at the time right before orgasm, relax, let go, and expand your abdomen with your breath. Once you become more aware of when your breathing becomes faster, you can consciously breathe slower and more fully. This allows you to move the sexual excitement throughout your body instead of unconsciously going right past all those exquisite feelings and going "over the top." This deep belly breathing opens the channels to allow for a full-body orgasm. It will help you relax and at the same time build up the erotic sexual charge to higher and higher peaks.

TOUCH—IN ALL ITS FORMS

One of the keys to great erotic touch is that the giver's fingers must feel just as good, or better, than the receiver's body. Confusing? The next time you are sensually touching someone, focus on your own fingertips. Concentrate on putting a lot of energy into feeling ecstasy in your fingers. See whether your lover starts to moan. This is one of those times where it works to focus on yourself and still be reassured that you are giving a great experience to someone else!

Massaging your lover is one of the most erotic, pleasurable, and giving things you can do. Not only will it reduce her stress, but it will probably reduce yours, too. There are many great books and DVDs on the subject of massage. *The Lover's Massage Kit* by Melanie Linn is a wonderful deck of cards that will teach you erotic massage techniques to please your lover. It is well worth your while to learn to give great massages. You can do it as a couple, and then practice on each other!

Beyond massage, most everyone wants to know about those special places—those places that you don't often think about that need love, healing touch, and erotic awakening. The following list provides some suggestions for those body parts and areas that might be forgotten or never thought about. This list can be expanded to include the places you like best, and it may even ignite some new, sensually sizzling spots you never before imagined.

- The inside of the thighs, where the leg meets the torso, are often tight, especially in women who are a bit anxious about sex. Using firm, small circles, massage this junction from the front of the body to the area of the buttocks. This will soften the muscle structures and stimulate the lymphatic system serving the pelvis.

- Anywhere there is hair on the body, it was put there for you to play with! Hair follicle ends are buried under the skin and meet the nerve endings to produce sensations that, if touched with sensuous, aware fingertips, will send a lover over the edge of pleasure. If you run your fingers through their hair as if you were the one feeling the pleasure, you are sure to please your partner.

- There are particular areas under the arms and down the sides of the torso that contain important lymph nodes that aid in our health. These also happen to be very erotic areas for touching and caressing. Start under the arms, and press the area with a medium firm touch, gently probing the fleshy hollow and surrounding tissue. Next, stroke the area with a smooth, firm touch and glide the hands slowly down the sides of the body to just above the waist. Repeat several times or more, each time getting more sensual than the last. This adds a stimulating effect to the lymph nodes and awakens receptivity. The sides of the body, from the underarms to the waist, is where the woman gets held in rear-entry positions and thus brings out more of her feline, animal-like nature!

> *"One of the most exquisitely erotic times my husband and I ever had was a ritual bathing that he set up for me. He drew the bath, added rose petals and bubbles, brought champagne, and strawberries, and put my favorite music on. After soaking and sipping, he washed me so tenderly all over, which was so incredibly sensuous. I had several orgasms that evening!"*
> *—Jennifer, 35*

- A man's penis is only partially exposed. At least a third of it is buried under his skin. To check this out, kneel down, naked, and place your hand behind and under your scrotum and feel for the lower third of your penis that is buried under the skin. No need to be erect. You should be able to feel it and even stroke it with enough lubrication. Can you tell whether you are more sensitive on the upper or under part of the buried area of your penis? You may need to be aroused for this. The lower third of the penis that is buried under the skin has the prostate gland at its very base. This is a highly pleasurable area, so don't neglect it. Ask your lover to pay some attention to this area the next time you are making love. She can reach it, with her hand, during oral sex, rear-entry positions, and some frontal positions, too.

- Pay attention to your lover's ears. Caress, suck, lick, and gently bite the earlobes, behind the ears, and where they attach to the neck. Women should use their fingernails to lightly scratch behind his ears and around the earlobes. This is a very erotic area of the body and sensually underutilized.

- Run your fingertips gently over your partner's eyes, starting from the center and moving outward. Your eyelids are supersensitive and we rarely think of touching them. Men are very visual, so their eyes take in a lot of their world. This kind of touch evokes love, caring, and a soothing tenderness that can put anyone into purring mode.

- Brush his ecstatic sexual energy up from his genitals, past his belly, to his heart area with one hand while lovemaking. This will spread his pleasure throughout his body and help him master his excitement. Moving the sexual energy into a man's heart is where *you* want it and where he will want it to prolong his pleasure. Very Tantric!

- When the man is on top, the woman should wrap her legs around him so that her heels put pressure on his sciatic notch, the area just above his hip joints. He'll get an acupressure massage while you're rocking and rolling. This relieves lower back pain and gives the woman an anchor for her ecstatic pleasure.

- Very slowly touch and caress your lover's face as lightly as you possibly can, barely touching it at all. Light touch allows your partner to focus on each exquisite detail coming from your fingertips. Often men want sexual touch to be strong and on the firmer side, but if you offer him up something different he'll understand the stimulating effects of subtle touch, too. Caressing the face is an erotic way to say that you love and care for your partner.

- Tickle and play with his feet by kissing and caressing them. Then lick between his toes and surprise him by taking one or two into your mouth and sucking deeply. He'll go over the top! Our feet are very sensitive, and this is a fantastic place on which to focus to take him off guard and give him a night he'll remember.

- Find a small child's blow-up swimming pool, put down a tarp, get out some older towels, and braid your hair if it's long. Warm up 3 cups of olive oil, put 1 to 2 cups in the bottom of the pool, undress, and the two of you get in. Add more warm oil if needed later, and then proceed to rub your body over every part of your lover's body! This will cover 99 places to touch and then some for over-the-top fun!

9

Potions, Rituals, and Love Essentials

"Leaves caught as they fall from trees
and powdered with peacock-bone and
fragments of a corpse's winding-sheet
will, when dusted lightly on the penis,
bewitch any woman living."

**—Part 7, Chapter 1, Verse 26,
the *Kama Sutra***

The final part of the *Kama Sutra* is devoted to making yourself attractive to the object of your desire and the uses of tonics or love potions to increase virility and arousal. The five senses were highly regarded in the *Kama Sutra*, and they were used to enhance the experiences of lovemaking and ritual. Lovemaking was considered excellent for one's health, vitality, and development. To that end, the experience of lovemaking encompassed the use of many substances, practices, and pleasuring rituals.

APHRODISIACS OF THE *KAMA SUTRA*

From dried monkey dung to mangoes, stinging insects to honey-laced milk, remedies in the *Kama Sutra* provide answers for many of the ailments that people have suffered throughout history. Erectile problems, low libido, shyness, attractiveness, winning a lover—all of these things and more were just as important then as they are today. The *Kama Sutra* even covers surgical procedures to improve a man's ability to be a very exotic lover!

POTENCY AND VIRILITY

The recipe provided at the beginning of the chapter, and many more that are included in the original *Kama Sutra*, are folk remedies that were used to enslave a lover that was not heeding to your advances. More subtle recipes are used today. Wouldn't you rather drink a little champagne and eat oysters than dust your penis with powdered peacock bone? These things may work, though. Sometimes we never really know what the ingredients are in modern remedies, either!

Potency and virility were important men of the ruling class because they tended to have several, or more, wives. It became an important issue to be able to pleasure all of them. Wives didn't like to be ignored or left unsatisfied, so male lovers were always looking for that extra something to keep them going.

It isn't what you've got but how you use it! Nevertheless, some learned men from ancient societies still wanted a bigger penis. One of the *Kama Sutra*'s remedies suggested, "By rubbing it successively with the juice of ashvagandha, or shabara roots, or jala shuka, or brihati, or buffalo butter, or hastikarna, or vajracalli, the penis will stay swollen for one month" (part 7, chapter 2, verse 28). Today, of course, you know better! Uh, perhaps you don't, but regardless, this stuff looks painful and sounds unsavory, but go ahead and see whether you can find the ingredients to try some of these aphrodisiacs.

> *"It's easier today to find aphrodisiacs that really work. We both take supplements and one of the side effects of one of them, 5-HTP, which we use for sleeping better, is what makes my boyfriend last a really long time when we're having intercourse. It's fantastic! He's like the energizer bunny."*
>
> *–Andrea, 27*

THE POWER OF ANCIENT AND MODERN APHRODISIACS

Studies have shown some interesting correlations between the scents that arouse men and women. In one study, combinations of aromas were compared for penile arousal in men. The conclusion was that smelling pumpkin pie spices increased the average man's erection by 40 percent.

Vanilla, lavender, and flower essences have been used for thousands of years to add allure to our already present bodily scents. Many of the tropical forests in Hawaii were cut down in the eighteenth and nineteenth centuries for the delicate scent of sandalwood. Its wood carries a musky, earthy scent that the finest European fans were made from. This wood never loses its scent, so it served as a perfume when a woman seductively fanned herself.

One food that has been proven to possess aphrodisiac qualities is chocolate. One of the active ingredients in chocolate produces phenylethylamine, the chemical the body manufactures when we fall in love. These chemical messengers speed up the flow of information that travels between our nerve endings. Phenylethylamine is similar in many ways to amphetamine, which dilates the blood vessels and creates energy and focus. It is not by chance that chocolate is so highly associated with love.

When the conquistadors invaded Mexico, Montezuma was reported to have drunk up to 50 cups a day of chocolate with chile and spices in it. He had to keep his stamina up to satisfy his many wives. Some women, as their hormonal balance shifts, crave chocolate as an unconscious remedy to lift their spirits and erotic arousal.

Foods that mimic the shape of the phallus or the vulva have always been considered aphrodisiacs. Cucumbers, eggplants, orchids, bananas, and oysters—these all have reputations as aphrodisiacs. Spanish fly (actually, it's a beetle!) soma—a drink prepared by pressing juice from the stalks of a certain mountain plant from ancient Asiatic cultures—and many Amazonian plants have long had reputations for their erotic powers. There are supplements out today that have some of these ingredients in them.

Some spices, seasonings, and foods with certain amino acids are good for getting the "heat" to rise in us. Adding a variety of spices to your food concoctions can have the wonderful effect of heightening arousal. Pumpkin pie spices, licorice, cinnamon, peppermint, curries, coriander, cardamom, lavender, chile peppers, sesame seeds, saffron, nutmeg, and pepper have qualities that aid in arousal. They are generally also very good for your health and vitality. But don't eat too much. Overeating will cause the opposite effect and dull the senses.

> "Sometimes I'll use a cock ring when I want to last a long time. It also makes me feel bigger than I am, or at least more swollen. They work great and I love it when my wife puts it on me. It's very erotic!"
> —Darren, 41

ARTIFICIAL PHALLUSES AND PENIS AUGMENTATIONS

The sex toys of today would either make an ancient Indian blush, or be very happy! Artificial phalluses were used fairly extensively by men loving women and by women loving women, too. They were strapped on with leather stings that wrapped around the waist of the man or woman to hold them in place. The carved phalluses were often inscribed with magical charms and spells.

The *Kama Sutra* goes into great detail about additions the man can have inserted into the foreskin of his penis. A young man would first perforate his penis and then stand in water until the bleeding stopped. He should then make love several times a day for several days so the wound won't heal. He should wash it with various ointments to keep it clean for several weeks and then he should proceed to widen the hole with objects designed for that use. Many types of items were then used to insert into the hole. Usually the lover would choose these, to her preference. They could be tubular, triangular, knobby, pointed, or round. The penis could then be adjusted, over the years, to larger and larger objects.

BRINGING OUR SENSES TO LOVEMAKING

Are you familiar with the scent of your lover? Have you ever consciously smelled him or her? Have you run your nose sensually along your lover's arm and even under her arm, sniffing as you go? Have you licked his sun-kissed skin after an afternoon of swimming in the ocean? Have you ever plucked a fresh rose petal and slowly caressed your lover's or even your own cheek with it? If you haven't, you are missing a whole treasure trove of senses, emotions, and feelings.

"Slow down and smell the roses" is an old saying, indeed, but in this fast-paced, contemporary existence of ours, the way to make time stop, or at least move more slowly, is to consciously absorb the world around us. You learn to understand and appreciate more aspects of life by modifying your speed. When lovemaking is slowed down, new worlds open up. Your senses come alive, and your freedom to play blossoms.

You usually aren't aware of your senses in your moment-to-moment perception. When you bring your senses to the forefront during sensuous time together and sexual play, the same old activities can suddenly take on new pleasure. When you really look deeply at you lover, feel her soft skin and silky hair, smell the subtle vapor rising from his body, or thrill at his power and gentleness, you are truly present to each other, together in a world of your own.

TOUCHING AND EROGENOUS ZONES

Touching consciously and receiving conscious touch is a learned experience. We aren't used to being lavished with a lot of touch. Can you imagine ten hands giving you a sensual massage? You'd probably protest that you just couldn't receive that amount of attention or stimulation. However, you are capable of receiving consciousness-altering touch, and probably much more than you ever dreamed of, but it takes practice.

Your skin is the largest organ of your body. It is also the largest erogenous zone. It's divided into three distinct areas: the primary, secondary, and tertiary zones. The tertiary zone is everything covered with thick masses of hair, such as your head, under your arms, and your pubic area. The more hair that exists on top of the skin, the fewer the nerve endings buried under the skin. One advantage of having hair is that each of those hair follicles comes into contact with a nerve beneath the skin. When you enliven an erogenous zone in a tertiary area, such as when you massage your lover's head, you are stimulating the nerve endings. Try gently grabbing a fistful of your partner's hair and pulling on it during the heights of passion, so that he or she experiences this pure sensation and potent arousal.

> "When my boyfriend comes to me fresh and clean, with no cologne or anything, and we begin to make love, his body gives off this wonderful natural scent that I love. Our aromas mix and change as we make love, like we're in a cloud of sex smells enveloping our bodies."
>
> —Tara, 32

Your secondary erogenous zones include most of your skin that has lighter amounts of hair on it. Places like your arms, legs, and torso feel great when you stroke and lightly rub them, but generally these areas require longer strokes to stimulate. The amount of nerve endings are fewer and are located farther apart in these areas, as are the hair follicles, so it takes more intense touch to generate the full, erotic experience.

"When my lover strokes my body, he sometimes uses massage oil, honey dust, or even a feather— making me all the more sensitive to his sensual touch."

–Dee, 30

The erogenous areas in the primary zone are the places on the body most easily aroused. Those are the lips, the ears, the genitals, and the palms of your hands and soles of your feet. These areas have little or no hair. They do have the largest concentration of nerve endings of any areas on the body, though. The lips and genitals are also mucous membranes, so they tend to be very wet and moist.

These three types of erogenous zones give you opportunities to explore touching in many different ways, whether you are being intimate or not. Keep this in mind when you are making love. Take advantage of the qualities of each area. For instance, you wouldn't want to erotically scratch your lover on the lips, but you might want to do so on the back or even the head. Running your fingers through your lover's hair is extremely sensual and can be done any time, not just in the bedroom.

You can suck, bite, blow, lick, and kiss any of these arousal points, though the intensity you use should vary depending on the area. Running an ice cube down his back is going to feel very different from putting it in your mouth while you are giving your lover fellatio. Smoothing a thick, luxuriant lubricant on your lover's vagina is going to feel different from using the same pressure, stroke speed, and substance on her arm. Stimulating touch of erogenous zones will heighten arousal, which, of course, leads to sizzling lovemaking!

SMELL AND TASTE

Your sense of smell informs your sense of taste. These two senses are intricately involved in bonding partners in the early stages of romance. There are scents you can consciously smell and ones you can't, such as pheromones, and both play large roles in whom you choose to love. Recall a time when you were repelled by someone's smell. Not a bad smell, just one you couldn't relate to. Now recall someone's smell that really turned you on. You really wanted to kiss (taste) her, right?

Considerable research has been conducted on the role of scent in mating and attachment. There is a special area in the nose that has receptors for pheromones, and it is wired directly to the inner brain. Pheromones and male and female hormones either repel or attract you toward another. Scent is the primary way that most animals recognize their mates and offspring. Subtle scent difference is how a baby lamb recognizes its mom in a field of a hundred other ewes.

Smell and taste are how you know that something is good for you to eat, to drink, to plant in your garden, and to love. These senses play a major role in your sexuality and are factors that influence you when choosing a lover. Special foods and aromas are conducive to lovemaking and sensual activities.

"A while back, my husband mentioned that my lips were probably the softest, most erotic part of my body. He asked me to pout and I wet my lips and stuck them out softly and all of a sudden I turned myself on! Ever since that time I am very aware of them and use them generously, all over his body!"
—Laurel, 37

HEARING AND SOUND

Music, the breeze in a willow tree, and the babbling of a brook are sounds that evoke a sensuous feeling. They can infuse you with an otherworldly sense that is a perfect, inspired background for lovemaking and intimacy. With the wide variety of music available today, you can micromanage your moods through your selection of music. Use music to help you in your sensual pursuits. Mystical, moody, classical, pop, jazz, blues, country love songs, even hip-hop—these all have a place in the bedroom, depending on the mood you want to set.

Everyone wants to hear words of love. Telling your lover how much you love him or her is one of the most endearing acts between lovers. It is essential. Equally important is the act of listening and hearing the other. Hearing requires active participation. Laugh a lot and say playful things to your partner. Give away words of love generously.

Use sexy words liberally, too. For both men and women, words can be powerful, erotic stimulators. In general, men prefer lusty, teasing, and more explicitly sexual language. Women tend to respond to more indirect language in the form of hints, words of love and desire, innuendo, and compliments. Regardless of what you like, start the erotic play before you get to the bedroom. The longer you are aroused, the stronger your responses will be when you get to the good stuff.

SIGHT

Sight is our most powerful sense by far. It is the first thing that registers with the brain when we have an experience. It overrides our other senses, sometimes with disastrous consequences. It's often said that men are very visual, but in truth, women are, too. When it comes to turn-ons and erotic imagery, the sense of sight is important to everyone.

Make your bedroom a sensuous place you really want to be. Clear up clutter and keep it neat. Specialists in the art of feng shui recommend that you not have exercise equipment, family pictures (such as your mom and dad next to your bed looking over at you), laundry baskets, and televisions in the bedroom. You can create a love temple in your bedroom with a few items that you can put away when not in use, and then bring out when it's time to create the love nest.

You can fashion a visual feast of yourself, too. Have a special wardrobe that you only bring out to tempt and seduce: a slinky nightgown, a sheer sarong, a lace teddy, a feather boa, a fan, and always a big smile. Men can look so sexy wearing a sarong, silk boxers, or a silk robe to entice her into a rendezvous with him in the bedroom.

Try making love with some of your lingerie still on. It is pretty hot to look up at your woman riding you in the sexy, low-cut lace bra you picked out for her last birthday. Imagine the fun if your man wears that velvet thong you gave him to bed. While you're peeling them to the side to give him fellatio, he's wide-eyed at the sensual feel of the string caressing his buttocks and the freeing of his penis while the velvet still cups his balls. How does that look to you? And there's nothing like the slinky sliding of silk on silk, and how it shows curves, bulges, and wetness. Sometimes it almost feels like it's not there at all.

A RITUAL OF THE SENSES

This is a ritual or love ceremony that you can use many times in your life. You can get experimental, adventurous, and edgy as you explore the possibilities and add your own ideas. Expand your capacity for touch, experience, eroticism, pleasure, and love by adapting and using the basic principles often.

PREPARATION

Set aside an evening, perhaps weeks ahead, to make love for an extended period of time. This will be a special evening, so you may want to save it for an occasion that is coming up—or not. It can be an occasion all its own, too. Send a love letter to your partner that invites him or her to this special evening. Find a card or create one that is sexy, sensual, and inviting. Be mysterious.

The day of the ritual, arrange small amounts of several sensual fruits, such as kiwis, grapes, and mangoes, on a beautiful plate with bits of dark chocolate, preferably with soft centers. Chill some champagne or sweet wine or a very good fruit juice. Find some mint, thyme, and blossoms from your garden, a single gardenia flower, or some sprigs of basil. You want things that provide an elegant and sensual aroma and taste. If you have an atomizer at home, put some lavender, rose, amber, or other essential oil in it, but not too much! There will be so much to sample . . .

"My boyfriend, Kevin, asked to give me a sensual evening and what an evening it was! His touch was amazing and he brought candles and music and lotions and oils and fur to touch me with. He treated me as a goddess. By the time he touched my clitoris with his tongue, I was already climaxing."

—Melissa, 41

Pick out several pieces of music that are erotic and arousing, yet soothing. A chime or bell, struck softly, can provide an interesting sensation when it is unexpected. Find a piece of velvet, a feather, a soft brush, a rose, a piece of silk, or any other items that will be sensual to the touch. Maybe something warm, like hot stones, and something cold, like ice, can be added to your box of tricks.

Think about all of the five senses of smell, taste, touch, sound, and sight, and have at least two things that evoke each of them. Since we are very visual beings and tend to let sight run over all of our other senses, use a small scarf as a blindfold, to take sight away for a while. Gather it all together: wine glasses, candles, massage oil, lubricant, and anything else that you're going to need later. Set these things aside on something beautiful.

SETTING THE MOOD

If you will be bathing each other before your ritual, prepare the bathroom with candles and sweet soaps. Fill the tub with warm water lightly scented with an essential oil and strew rose petals on the water. Light some candles.

When the hour has arrived, and you are arrayed in slinky silk, or nothing at all, invite your lover into the bath. With a soft cloth or sponge, lavish attention on every part while gazing lovingly into his or her eyes. Drizzle warm water from a sponge upon both nipples, and then lick them lustfully. Kiss whatever peeks out of the water. Kiss, kiss, and kiss some more. Wrap your legs around your lover's waist and fondle each other as you wash your delicate parts. Finish with warm, fresh water over your glistening skin, and then step into big, soft towels so that you can dry each other erotically.

Rule of Love

You can create a dramatic room by draping a red scarf over the lamp next to your bed, but remember to put it over a safe shade that will keep it from coming into contact with the bulb. Include extra pillows, arrange some statues, and drape scarves in strategic places. Put a few drops of an essential oil on the light bulb for an even more dramatic effect.

THE EXPERIENCE

Once you are both in the bedroom, where candles are lit and music is softly playing in the background, sit facing each other for a few minutes and simply gaze into one another's eyes. Breathe together while gazing into the windows of your souls. After a few minutes, gently ask your partner whether there is anything to clear up that may be between you. Listen lovingly, and then do the same. Keep it simple, but do clear up any issue that seems even slightly negative or confusing. You don't want it to come up later.

Lie down with your partner and in a beautiful way say how much you love her. Ask if you may put the blindfold on your lover, and with consent, gently tie it over her eyes and make her comfortable. Taking away the sense of vision will enhance your lover's other sensual experiences, so reassure and connect with her with light touch. Tease and titillate your lover's senses.

Begin with smell. Pass a piece of fruit slowly under your lover's nose and ask whether he can tell you what it is. Be playful. Don't offer a taste until there have been a few guesses, and then gently and erotically place it in his mouth. You can even tease a little by stroking it on the tongue and around the lips before giving it to eat. Offer another piece of food with a different smell and taste. Dip your fingers into your drink and drop some sweet liquid onto your blindfolded partner's tongue. Allow your lover to suck your fingers.

Select a feather or a soft brush next. Lightly brush the very tips of the nipples. Pause, and then do it again. Drag it down the arm and brush the insides of the elbows, where it bends. Blow on the sensitive place there, and then continue to the fingertips and outward. Kiss the palms. Draw the feather through the valleys of the arms and legs and blow on those places as you do. Now take a piece of fur or silk and lightly caress the face, throat, and chest, with special attention to the erect nipples. Run your fingernails exquisitely slowly down the arm to the fingertips, pinch the nipples according to your lover's liking, and follow immediately with a long stroke of the fur.

Now that your torturously delicious touch has your lover reaching for more, drag the fur through the folds of the thighs again and again, just barely missing the genitals. Brush the tiny hairs with your fingers, but don't touch the skin! Blow your hot breath on his swelling penis or her moist clitoris.

Rule of Love

Men, notice and appreciate her efforts to be beautiful for you. Don't get her hair wet or wash away her makeup! Turn her on and save the teasing and hot, sticky, wild undoing for later!

Every once and in a while, touch yourself as well. Pleasure your skin with fur and fingers; this is for you, too. Moan when you feel it, and breathe in your lover's ear. Brush his or her face with your face, dusting the chest with your hair.

Continue with your other erotic items. Crush a cream-filled chocolate on your lover's nipple, and then eat it off. Pour a teaspoon of warm honey into the navel, and suck it out. Lie on top of your lover and brush your body all over his body. Kiss his penis or her clitoris, just once. Offer your nipples and fingers or even your clitoris, just for a moment, to his or her seeking mouth. Tap her nipples with the tip of your penis. Tap her clitoris, then move away and lick her nipples. Give his penis a little squeeze, even a lick, and then breathe sensuously on it.

The possibilities are endless. Make this ritual last by teasing and coaxing sensual pleasure out of your partner until cries of longing and desire drown out the music. Be playful, erotic, and sensuous. Let your imagination run wild. Sing and whisper words of love into his ear. Wax poetic about her beauty, and speak of your amazement at how aroused you are. Go back to furs and silks, feathers and fingertips, always with more licking and sucking. Let the rhythm rise, until . . . until . . . When all is quiet, remove the blindfold and spend some time gazing into one another's eyes and feeding each other fruit and kisses.

Rule of Love

In truth, your brain is your greatest erogenous zone. Tease, hint, touch, and stimulate leading up to your big night, so the sexual tension will be high. Set the tone for the evening by dropping little hints throughout the days leading up to the evening. Be sensual, but don't make love for a few nights beforehand so you can build the anticipation slowly.

THE BEGINNINGS AND ENDINGS OF LOVE

"Lovers will find that if they dally with each other in pleasing ways and so create confidence in each other, both at the commencement and at the end of congress, they will heighten the love between them."
—Part 2, Chapter 10, Verse 23, the Kama Sutra

The attention to love is more important today than ever before. Love is a sanctuary in a world that is increasingly more urbanized and fragmented. For millennia, India and other Asian countries had love manuals to school them both romantically and sexually, with some of these booklets still in exist today to inform modern people. As deep and wise as these cultures were it is obvious that each culture, in its own time, must create the information that is wise for its own people. That is why the writers of the Love sutras left them short and to the point—so that they could be interpreted by each generation, throughout time.

Many discoveries have been made in the fields of health, sexual sciences, biology and neurology in recent years. When you combine these natural sciences with what is known from cultures past whole new fields open to the modern seeker. Our knowledge of the body adds to the body of knowledge the ancient love explorers knew. That is the beauty of the *Kama Sutra*—its timelessness allows for expanded learning and loving through the eyes and understanding of current wisdom. *The Rules of Love* can then benefit all who seek to increase their skills and deeply understand the importance of love and sexuality in their life.

The Rules of Love says that techniques should be learned by those who are inspired by them, but, in the end, the acts of love are naturally acquired and are practiced at will by both lovers. The most important aspects of lovemaking that you can master are being present with your partner and touching her in the sensual ways that she loves to be touched. Techniques, new positions, different locations, love toys—all these things make love interesting and create the variety that keeps lovemaking fresh and alive. It is the caring, though—the tenderness and the willingness to explore and play with your lover—that is the true inspiration of love.

Acknowledgments

I am in gratitude to my many teachers and mentors I have been blessed to have in my life. They include, but are not limited to, my mother and father Bette and Mel Cox, my husband Michael Heumann and our three fantastic daughters, Amira Ludwig-Conklin, Nicole Heumann, and Dawn Heumann. I have been graced to study with and know, as friends and mentors, many wonderful Tantra teachers over the years: Charles and Caroline Muir, Johanina Wikoff, Lori Grace Starr, Margot Anand, Shinzo Fugimaki, Susan Campbell, and the late Robert Frey. Special thanks to Diane Conn Darling for her support, erotic ideas, and editing. I am in deep appreciation to the contemporary sexuality researchers who are navigating the intersections between physiology, brain chemistry, neurology, and somatic embodiment. High praise, great blessings, and a deep thank you to all of you!

Suzie Heumann is an author, writer, columnist, radio personality and producer of instructional videos on the subjects of The *Kama Sutra*, Tantra, and other sexual disciplines since 1987. She currently runs the Internet sites www.Tantra.com and www.Tantra.org as President/CEO of LLL Media Group, Inc. She has co-produced three instructional videos on Tantra and the Kama Sutra: "Ancient Secrets of Sexual Ecstasy," "Multi Orgasmic Response Ecstasy Training for Women," and the "Multi Orgasmic Response Ecstasy Training for Men." These films have involved many of the world's best-known teachers of Western Tantra. Suzie is the author of two previous books: *The Everything Great Sex Book* and *The Everything Kama Sutra Book*. She lives in Sebastopol, CA.

Index